THE GRIDIRON UK GUIDE TO

AMERICAN FOOTBALL

All-Time Greats

D0551842

THE GRIDIRON UK GUIDE TO

AMERICAN FOOTBALL
All-Time Greats

ROSS BIDDISCOMBE

Patrick Stephens, Wellingborough

First published in 1986

British Library Cataloguing in Publication Data

Biddiscombe, Ross
American football all-time greats.
1. Football players – Biography
I. Title
796.332'092'2   GV939.A1

ISBN 0-85059-894-X

*Patrick Stephens Limited is part of the
Thorsons Publishing Group*

Printed and bound in Great Britain

Contents

Introduction	7	Jack Lambert	95
The All-Pros	9	Dick Lane	100
		Bob Lilly	104
Lyle Alzado	17	Vince Lombardi	107
Sammy Baugh	21	Sid Luckman	112
Raymond Berry	25	John Madden	116
George Blanda	29	Bronko Nagurski	120
Terry Bradshaw	33	Joe Namath	124
Jim Brown	38	Pete Pihos	131
Dick Butkus	43	John Riggins	135
Earl (Dutch) Clark	48	Jim Ringo	141
Larry Csonka	52	Gayle Sayers	145
Art Donovan	57	O. J. Simpson	149
Otto Graham	61	Ken Stabler	155
Red Grange	65	Bart Starr	160
George Halas	69	Roger Staubach	165
Franco Harris	74	Jan Stenerud	169
Elroy Hirsch	79	Fran Tarkenton	174
Sam Huff	84	Jim Thorpe	179
Don Hutson	88	Johnny Unitas	183
David 'Deacon' Jones	91	Paul Warfield	188

Acknowledgements

Just like the speech of an Oscar-winner, my list of credits seems long, but all are very special.

The Pro Football Hall of Fame in Canton, Ohio, has provided much inspiration, facts and pictures. I'm deeply indebted to Don Smith and Anne Magnus for their assistance.

Vernon Biever's photographs are an outstanding contribution to this work. His trust and interest have been invaluable. Paul Spinelli has also come up with his usual excellent pics.

The 28 National Football League clubs have all provided assistance in some way, either great or small. Also, fellow hack Barry Stanton has sometimes appeared to be a human dictionary of football facts.

On this side of the Atlantic, I'd like to thank Sue Weekes for her typing, Kelly Healy for Dutch Clark, Bev Wills, all at *Gridiron UK* in particular and Special Publications Division in general for their help and tolerance, Maizie and Harry for 'America', my parents, John and Joyce, for their encouragement and, last but not least, Jacqueline for her subbing, smiling and everything else.

Introduction

Who were the greatest players in the history of pro football? Who were the best coaches? Who were the most naturally gifted? Who overcame the greatest obstacles?

These are questions which cross the minds of football fans everywhere in the world. In modern times, the gridiron game has such a high-profile in the media that the players of this era seem to be elevated to superstardom almost before a pass is caught or a tackle made. Only time will tell whether that over-used word 'great' will ever sit comfortably next to their names.

There have been over sixty years of professional football and no one man has been able to see all the players who've graced the gridiron during that time. So everyone has their own personal favourites among those who've come under the spotlight. The 39 men in this book are my favourites and are here for a number of reasons. Some have incredible stories of dedication, others were simply super-human athletes, all had a major impact on football. The 39 cover every decade of the game from the twenties to the eighties. They cover just about all positions, on the field and off. They colour the walls of young boys' bedrooms and the memories of old men.

The expanding world of American football needs to recall such tales of bravery, courage, ingenuity, artistry and athleticism which are woven into the careers of these legends.

Each year new fans become enthralled with this ultimate sport, but the men they believe to be heroes today must be judged against the proven heroes of yesterday — heroes like the 39 in this book. To choose so few great men to write about is the toughest cut I have ever had to make. Without a time machine to take me back, I have seen too few of these men play while others I have met only in their retirement. Yet all their stories should be read, re-told and marvelled at because they shaped the game into what it is today. And, though each one of them is now a retired statistic and memory, it is at times like this, during the interminably-long, off-season, that they come alive again. The great players of pro football only retire from the field of play, never from the field of the imagination.

Ross Biddiscombe, May 1986

The All-Pros

Players have good years, players have bad years. But great players have great decades. Consistent excellence is the mark of the best as against the very good. At the end of each decade, a selection committee at Pro Football's Hall of Fame in Canton, Ohio, decides on the men who would fill a dream team from the past ten years. Sixty years of pro football has produced six All-Pro teams brimming with star names of the NFL. The rise and fall of the American Football League was also marked by a dream team compiled from the days before it merged with the NFL.

Thirty-two of the 39 men in this book made the various all-star teams, others might make the team of the eighties. Just eighteen players were selected for the team of the twenties, but the growth of the sport meant that 47 men were needed to fill the squad of the seventies. Gone were the days of the eleven-man team when players turned out on both offense and defense. Nowadays teams have 45-man rosters and even the dream teams need to get bigger. Players featured in this book are highlighted in bold type.

The Twenties

Name	Position	Height ft/in	Weight (lb)	Years in League	Teams
Guy Chamberlain	End	6-2	210	1920-27	Chicago Bears, Canton Bulldogs, Frankford Yellowjackets, Chicago Cardinals, Cleveland Bulldogs
Lavern Dilweg	End	6-3	203	1926-34	Green Bay Packers, Milwaukee Badgers
George Halas	**End**	**6-1**	**180**	**1920-29**	**Chicago Bears**
Ed Healey	Tackle	6-3	196	1920-27	Rock Island Independents, Chicago Bears
Pete (Fats) Henry	Tackle	6-0	250	1920-23, 1925-28	Canton Bulldogs, Akron Steels, New York Giants, Pottsville Maroons
Cal Hubbard	Tackle	6-5	250	1927-33, 1935-36	New York Giants, Green Bay Packers, Pittsburgh Pirates
Steve Owen	Tackle	6-2	235	1924-31, 1933	Kansas City Cowboys, New York Giants
Heartley (Hunk) Anderson	Guard	5-11	195	1922-25	Chicago Bears
Walt Kiesling	Guard	6-2	245	1926-38	Duluth Eskimos, Pottsville Maroons, Chicago Cardinals, Chicago Bears, Green Bay Packers, Pittsburgh Pirates

Name	Position	Height ft/in	Weight (lb)	Years in League	Teams
Mike Michalske	Guard	6-0	210	1927-35, 1937	New York Yankees, Green Bay Packers
George Trafton	Center	6-2	235	1920-32	Chicago Bears
Jimmy Conzelman	Back	6-0	180	1920-29	Decatur Staleys, Rock Island Independents, Milwaukee Badgers, Detroit Panthers, Providence Steamrollers
John (Paddy) Driscoll	Back	5-11	170	1920-29	Chicago Cardinals, Chicago Bears
Harold (Red) Grange	**Back**	**6-1**	**190**	**1925-27, 1929-34**	**Chicago Bears, New York Yankees**
Joe Guyon	Back	6-1	180	1920-27	Canton Bulldogs, Cleveland Indians, Oorang Indians, Rock Island Independents, New York Giants, Rock Island Independents, New York Giants, Kansas City Cowboys
Earl (Curly) Lambeau	Back	6-0	195	1921-29	Green Bay Packers
Ernie Nevers	Back	6-1	205	1926-27, 1929-31	Duluth Eskimos, Chicago Cardinals
Jim Thorpe	**Back**	**6-1**	**190**	**1920-26, 1929**	**Canton Bulldogs, Cleveland Indians, Oorang Indians, Rock Island Independents, New York Giants, Toledo Maroons, Chicago Cardinals**

The Thirties

Name	Position	Height ft/in	Weight (lb)	Years in League	Teams
Bill Hewitt	End	5-11	195	1932-39, 1943	Chicago Bears, Philadelphia Eagles
Don Hutson	**End**	**6-1**	**180**	**1935-45**	**Green Bay Packers**
Wayne Millner	End	6-0	190	1936-41, 1945	Washington Redskins
Gaynell Tinsley	End	6-1	200	1937-38, 1940	Chicago Cardinals
George Christensen	Tackle	6-2	238	1931-38	Portsmouth Spartans, Detroit Lions
Frank Cope	Tackle	6-3	234	1938-47	New York Giants
Albert (Turk) Edwards	Tackle	6-2	256	1932-40	Washington Redskins
Bill Lee	Tackle	6-2	235	1935-42, 1946	Brooklyn Dodgers, Green Bay Packers
Joe Stydahar	Tackle	6-4	230	1936-42, 1945-46	Chicago Bears
Grover (Ox) Emerson	Guard	6-0	190	1931-38	Portsmouth Spartans, Detroit Lions, Brooklyn Dodgers
Danny Fortmann	Guard	6-0	207	1936-43	Chicago Bears
Charles (Buckets) Goldenberg	Guard	5-10	222	1933-45	Green Bay Packers
Russ Letlow	Guard	6-0	212	1936-42, 1946	Green Bay Packers
Mel Hein	Center	6-3	230	1931-45	New York Giants
George Svendsen	Center	6-4	240	1935-37, 1940-41	Green Bay Packers

Name	Position	Height ft/in	Weight (lb)	Years in League	Teams
Cliff Battles	Back	6-1	185	1932-37	Washington Redskins
Earl (Dutch) Clark	**Back**	**6-1**	**185**	**1931-32, 1934-38**	**Portsmouth Spartans, Detroit Lions**
Beattie Feathers	Back	5-11	177	1934-40	Chicago Bears, Brooklyn Dodgers, Green Bay Packers
Arnie Herber	Back	6-1	200	1930-40, 1944-45	Green Bay Packers, New York Giants
Clarke Hinkle	Back	5-11	201	1932-41	Green Bay Packers
Cecil Isbell	Back	6-0	190	1938-42	Green Bay Packers
Alphonse (Tuffy) Leemans	Back	6-0	200	1936-43	New York Giants
John (Johnny Blood) McNally	Back	6-1	190	1925-39	Milwaukee Badgers, Duluty Eskimos, Pottsville Maroons, Green Bay Packers, Pittsburg Pirates, Pittsburgh Steelers
Bronislaw (Bronko) Nagurski	**Back**	**6-2**	**230**	**1930-37, 1943**	**Chicago Bears**
Ken Strong	Back	5-11	210	1929-35, 1939, 1944-47	Staten Island Stapletons, New York Giants

The Forties

Jim Benton	End	6-3	210	1938-40, 1942-47	Cleveland Rams, Chicago Bears, Los Angeles Rams
Jack Ferrante	End	6-1	205	1941, 1944-50	Philadelphia Eagles
Ken Kavanaugh	End	6-3	205	1940-41, 1945-50	Chicago Bears
Dante Lavelli	End	6-0	192	1946-56	Cleveland Browns
Pete Pihos	**End**	**6-1**	**215**	**1947-55**	**Philadelphia Eagles**
Mac Speedie	End	6-3	205	1946-52	Cleveland Browns
Ed Sprinkle	End	6-1	207	1944-55	Chicago Bears
Al Blozis	Tackle	6-7	250	1942-44	New York Giants
George Connor	Tackle	6-3	240	1948-55	Chicago Bears
Frank Kilroy	Tackle	6-2	244	1943-55	Philadelphia Eagles
Buford (Baby) Ray	Tackle	6-6	250	1938-48	Green Bay Packers
Vic Sears	Tackle	6-3	236	1941-42, 1945-53	Philadelphia Eagles
Al Wistert	Tackle	6-1	214	1943-51	Philadelphia Eagles
Bruno Banducci	Guard	5-11	220	1944-54	Philadelphia Eagles, San Francisco 49ers
Bill Edwards	Guard	6-3	218	1940-42, 1946	New York Giants
Garrard (Buster) Ramsey	Guard	6-1	220	1946-51	Chicago Cardinals
Bill Willis	Guard	6-2	215	1946-53	Cleveland Browns
Len Younce	Guard	6-1	210	1941, 1943-44, 1946-48	New York Giants
Charles Brock	Center	6-2	210	1939-47	Green Bay Packers
Clyde (Bulldog) Turner	Center	6-2	240	1940-52	Chicago Bears
Alex Wojciechowicz	Center	6-0	235	1938-50	Detroit Lions, Philadelphia Eagles
Sammy Baugh	**Quarterback**	**6-2**	**185**	**1937-52**	**Washington Redskins**
Sid Luckman	**Quarterback**	**6-0**	**195**	**1939-50**	**Chicago Bears**

Name	Position	Height ft/in	Weight (lb)	Years in League	Teams
Bob Waterfield	Quarterback	6-2	200	1945-52	Cleveland Rams, Los Angels Rams
Tony Canadeo	Halfback	5-11	190	1941-44, 1946-52	Green Bay Packers
Bill Dudley	Halfback	5-10	175	1942, 1945-51, 1953	Pittsburgh Steelers, Detroit Lions, Washington Redskins
George McAfee	Halfback	6-0	180	1940-41, 1945-50	Chicago Bears
Charley Trippi	Halfback	6-0	185	1947-55	Chicago Cardinals
Steve Van Buren	Halfback	6-0	205	1944-51	Philadelphia Eagles
Byron (Whizzer) White	Halfback	6-1	188	1938, 1940-41	Pittsburgh Pirates, Detroit Lions
Marlin (Pat) Harder	Fullback	5-11	205	1946-53	Chicago Cardinals, Detroit Lions
Marion Motley	Fullback	6-1	238	1946-53, 1955	Cleveland Browns, Pittsburgh Steelers
Bill Osmanski	Fullback	5-11	200	1939-43, 1946-47	Chicago Bears

The Fifties

OFFENSE

Name	Position	Height ft/in	Weight (lb)	Years in League	Teams
Raymond Berry	**End**	**6-2**	**190**	**1955-67**	**Baltimore Colts**
Tom Fears	End	6-2	215	1948-56	Los Angeles Rams
Bobby Walston	End	6-0	195	1951-62	Philadelphia Eagles
Roosevelt Brown	Tackle	6-3	255	1953-65	New York Giants
Bob St. Clair	Tackle	6-9	265	1953-63	San Francisco 49ers
Richard Barwegan	Guard	6-1	228	1947-54	New York Yankees, Baltimore Colts, Chicago Bears
Jim Parker	Guard	6-3	275	1957-67	Baltimore Colts
Dick Stanfel	Guard	6-3	240	1952-58	Detroit Lions, Washington Redskins
Otto Graham	**Quarterback**	**6-1**	**195**	**1946-55**	**Cleveland Browns**
Bobby Layne	Quarterback	6-2	210	1948-62	Chicago Bears, New York Bulldogs, Detroit Lions, Pittsburgh Steelers
Norm Van Brocklin	Quarterback	6-1	202	1949-60	Los Angeles Rams, Philadelphia Eagles
Chuck Bednarik	Center	6-3	235	1949-62	Philadelphia Eagles
Lenny Moore	Flanker	6-1	190	1956-67	Baltimore Colts
Elroy (Crazy Legs) Hirsch	**Flanker**	**6-2**	**190**	**1946-57**	**Chicago Rockets, Los Angeles Rams**
Frank Gifford	Halfback	6-1	200	1952-60, 1962-64	New York Giants
Ollie Matson	Halfback	6-2	215	1952, 1954-66	Chicago Cardinals, Los Angeles Rams, Detroit Lions, Philadelphia Eagles
Hugh McElhenny	Halfback	6-1	190	1952-64	San Francisco 49ers, Minnesota Vikings, New York Giants, Detroit Lions
Alan Ameche	Fullback	6-1	220	1955-60	Baltimore Colts
Fletcher (Joe) Perry	Fullback	6-0	200	1948-62	San Francisco 49ers, Baltimore Colts
Lou Groza	Kicker	6-3	250	1946-59, 1961-67	Cleveland Browns

Name	Position	Height ft/in	Weight (lb)	Years in League	Teams
DEFENSE					
Gino Marchetti	End	6-4	245	1952-64, 1966	Dallas Texans, Baltimore Colts
Leonard Ford	End	6-5	258	1948-58	Los Angeles Dons, Cleveland Browns, Green Bay Packers
Art Donovan	**Tackle**	**6-3**	**270**	**1950-61**	**Baltimore Colts, New York Yankees, Dallas Texans**
Leo Nomellini	Tackle	6-3	262	1950-63	San Francisco 49ers
Ernie Stautner	Tackle	6-2	230	1950-63	Pittsburgh Steelers
Joe Fortunato	Linebacker	6-1	225	1955-66	Chicago Bears
Bill George	Linebacker	6-2	235	1952-66	Chicago Bears, Los Angeles Rams
Sam Huff	**Linebacker**	**6-1**	**230**	**1956-67**	**New York Giants, Washington Redskins**
Joe Schmidt	Linebacker	6-0	220	1953-65	Detroit Lions
Jack Butler	Halfback	6-1	193	1951-59	Pittsburgh Steelers
Dick (Night Train) Lane	**Halfback**	**6-2**	**200**	**1952-65**	**Los Angeles Rams, Chicago Cardinals, Detroit Lions**
Jack Christiansen	Safety	6-1	180	1951-58	Detroit Lions
Yale Lary	Safety	5-11	190	1952-53, 1956-64	Detroit Lions
Emlen Tunnell	Safety	6-1	210	1948-61	New York Giants, Green Bay Packers

The Sixties

Name	Position	Height ft/in	Weight (lb)	Years in League	Teams
OFFENSE					
Del Shofner	End	6-3	190	1957-67	Los Angeles Rams, New York Giants
Charley Taylor	End	6-3	210	1964-77	Washington Redskins
Bob Brown	Tackle	6-4	295	1964-68	Philadelphia Eagles
Forrest Gregg	Tackle	6-4	250	1956, 1958-71	Green Bay Packers, Dallas Cowboys
Ralph Neely	Tackle	6-6	265	1965-77	Dallas Cowboys
Gene Hickerson	Guard	6-3	260	1958-60, 1962-73	Cleveland Browns
Jerry Kramer	Guard	6-3	254	1958-68	Green Bay Packers
Howard Mudd	Guard	6-2	254	1964-70	San Francisco 49ers, Chicago Bears
Jim Ringo	**Center**	**6-2**	**230**	**1953-67**	**Green Bay Packers, Philadelphia Eagles**
Sonny Jurgensen	Quarterback	6-0	203	1957-74	Philadelphia Eagles, Washington Redskins
Bart Starr	**Quarterback**	**6-1**	**190**	**1956-71**	**Green Bay Packers**
John Unitas	**Quarterback**	**6-1**	**196**	**1956-72**	**Baltimore Colts**
Gary Collins	Flanker	6-4	215	1962-67	Cleveland Browns
Boyd Dowler	Flanker	6-5	225	1959-71	Green Bay Packers, Washington Redskins
John Mackey	Tight End	6-2	224	1963-72	Baltimore Colts, San Diego Chargers
John David Crow	Halfback	6-2	224	1958-68	Chicago Cardinals, St. Louis Cardinals, San Francisco 49ers
Paul Hornung	Halfback	6-2	215	1957-62, 1964-66	Green Bay Packers

Name	Position	Height ft/in	Weight (lb)	Years in League	Teams
Leroy Kelly	Halfback	6-0	200	1964-73	Cleveland Browns
Gale Sayers	**Halfback**	**6-0**	**198**	**1965-71**	**Chicago Bears**
Jim Brown	**Fullback**	**6-2**	**232**	**1957-65**	**Cleveland Browns**
Jim Taylor	Fullback	6-0	215	1958-67	Green Bay Packers, New Orleans Saints
Jim Bakken	Field Goal Kicker	6-0	200	1962-78	St. Louis Cardinals
Don Chandler	Punter	6-2	210	1956-67	New York Giants, Green Bay Packers

DEFENSE

Name	Position	Height ft/in	Weight (lb)	Years in League	Teams
Doug Atkins	End	6-8	270	1953-69	Cleveland Browns, Chicago Bears, New Orleans Saints
Willie Davis	End	6-3	245	1958-69	Cleveland Browns, Green Bay Packers
David (Deacon) Jones	**End**	**6-5**	**260**	**1961-74**	**Los Angeles Rams, San Diego Chargers, Washington Redskins**
Alex Karras	Tackle	6-2	245	1958-62, 1964-70	Detroit Lions
Bob Lilly	**Tackle**	**6-5**	**260**	**1961-74**	**Dallas Cowboys**
Merlin Olsen	Tackle	6-5	276	1962-76	Los Angeles Rams
Dick Butkus	**Linebacker**	**6-3**	**245**	**1965-73**	**Chicago Bears**
Larry Morris	Linebacker	6-2	220	1955-57, 1959-66	Los Angeles Rams, Chicago Bears, Atlanta Falcons
Ray Nitschke	Linebacker	6-3	240	1958-72	Green Bay Packers
Tommy Nobis	Linebacker	6-2	235	1966-76	Atlanta Falcons
Dave Robinson	Linebacker	6-3	240	1963-74	Green Bay Packers, Washington Redskins
Herb Adderley	Halfback	6-0	200	1961-72	Green Bay Packers, Dallas Cowboys
Lem Barney	Halfback	6-0	202	1967-77	Detroit Lions
Bob Boyd	Halfback	5-10	192	1960-68	Baltimore Colts
Ed Meador	Safety	5-11	199	1959-70	Los Angeles Rams
Larry Wilson	Safety	6-0	190	1960-72	St. Louis Cardinals
Willie Wood	Safety	5-10	160	1960-71	Green Bay Packers
Don Chandler	Punter	6-2	210	1956-67	New York Giants, Green Bay Packers

The Seventies

OFFENSE

Name	Position	Height ft/in	Weight (lb)	Years in League	Teams
Harold Carmichael	Wide Receiver	6-8	225	1971-83, 1984	Philadelphia Eagles, Dallas Cowboys
Drew Pearson	Wide Receiver	6-0	183	1973-83	Dallas Cowboys
Lynn Swann	Wide Receiver	6-0	180	1974-82	Pittsburgh Steelers
Paul Warfield	**Wide Receiver**	**6-0**	**188**	**1964-69, 1970-74, 1975, 1976-77**	**Cleveland Browns, Miami Dolphins, Memphis (WFL)**
Dave Casper	Tight End	6-4	230	1974-80, 1980-83	Oakland Raiders, Houston Oilers
Charlie Sanders	Tight End	6-4	230	1966-77	Detroit Lions
Dan Dierdorf	Tackle	6-3	288	1971-83	St. Louis Cardinals
Art Shell	Tackle	6-5	286	1968-82	Oakland Raiders

Name	Position	Height ft/in	Weight (lb)	Years in League	Teams
Rayfield Wright	Tackle	6-6	260	1967-79	Dallas Cowboys
Ron Yary	Tackle	6-6	255	1968-82	Minnesota Vikings
Joe DeLamielleure	Guard	6-3	245	1973-79, 1980-84	Buffalo Bills, Cleveland Browns
John Hannah	Guard	6-2	265	1973-85	New England Patriots
Larry Little	Guard	6-1	265	1967-68, 1969-80	San Diego Chargers, Miami Dolphins
Gene Upshaw	Guard	6-5	255	1967-82	Oakland Raiders
Jim Langer	Center	6-2	257	1970-80, 1980-81	Miami Dolphins, Minnesota Vikings
Mike Webster	Center	6-2	255	1974-	Pittsburgh Steelers
Terry Bradshaw	**Quarterback**	**6-3**	**215**	**1970-83**	**Pittsburgh Steelers**
Ken Stabler	**Quarterback**	**6-3**	**215**	**1970-79, 1980-81, 1982-84**	**Oakland Raiders, Houston Oilers, New Orleans Saints**
Roger Staubach	**Quarterback**	**6-3**	**197**	**1969-79**	**Dallas Cowboys**
Earl Campbell	Running Back	5-11	224	1978-	Houston Oilers, New Orleans Saints
Franco Harris	**Running Back**	**6-3**	**230**	**1972-83, 1984**	**Pittsburgh Steelers, Seattle Seahawks**
Walter Payton	Running Back	5-10	202	1975	Chicago Bears
O. J. Simpson	**Running Back**	**6-1**	**216**	**1969-77, 1978-79**	**Buffalo Bills, San Francisco 49ers**
Garo Yepremlan	Kicker	5-8	175	1966-67, 1970-78, 1979, 1980-81	Detroit Lions, Miami Dolphins, New Orleans Saints, Tampa Bay Buccaneers

DEFENSE

Name	Position	Height ft/in	Weight (lb)	Years in League	Teams
Carl Eller	End	6-6	247	1964-78, 1979	Minnesota Vikings, Seattle Seahawks
L.C. Greenwood	End	6-6	245	1969-81	Pittsburgh Steelers
Harvey Martin	End	6-5	250	1973-83	Dallas Cowboys
Jack Youngblood	End	6-4	244	1971-85	Los Angeles Rams
Joe Greene	Tackle	6-4	275	1969-81	Pittsburgh Steelers
Bob Lilly	**Tackle**	**6-5**	**260**	**1961-74**	**Dallas Cowboys**
Merlin Olsen	Tackle	6-5	270	1962-78	Los Angles Rams
Alan Page	Tackle	6-4	245	1967-78, 1978-81	Minnesota Vikings, Chicago Bears
Bobby Bell	Linebacker	6-4	228	1963-74	Kansas City Chiefs
Robert Brazile	Linebacker	6-4	238	1975-	Houston Oilers
Dick Butkus	**Linebacker**	**6-3**	**245**	**1965-73**	**Chicago Bears**
Jack Ham	Linebacker	6-1	225	1969-73	Baltimore Colts
Ted Hendricks	Linebacker	6-7	225	1969-73, 1974, 1975-83	Baltimore Colts, Green Bay Packers, Oakland Raiders
Jack Lambert	**Linebacker**	**6-4**	**220**	**1974-84**	**Pittsburgh Steelers**
Willie Brown	Cornerback	6-1	190	1963-66, 1967-78	Denver Broncos, Oakland Raiders
Jimmy Johnson	Cornerback	6-2	185	1961-76	San Francisco 49ers
Roger Wehrli	Cornerback	6-0	190	1969-82	St. Louis Cardinals
Louis Wright	Cornerback	6-2	200	1975-	Denver Broncos
Dick Anderson	Safety	6-2	196	1968-77	Miami Dolphins
Cliff Harris	Safety	6-1	192	1970-79	Dallas Cowboys
Ken Houston	Safety	6-3	198	1967-72, 1973-80	Houston Oilers, Washington Redskins
Larry Wilson	Safety	6-0	190	1960-73	St. Louis Cardinals
Ray Guy	Punter	6-3	195	1973-	Oakland Raiders

The AFL Team

Name	Position	Height ft/in	Weight (lb)	Years in League	Teams
OFFENSE					
Lance Alworth	Flanker	6-0	180	1962-70, 1971-72	San Diego Chargers, Dallas Cowboys
Don Maynard	End	6-1	179	1958, 1960-62, 1963-72	New York Giants, New York Titans, New York Jets
Fred Arbanas	Tight End	6-3	240	1962, 1963-70	Dallas Texans, Kansas City Chiefs
Ron Mix	Tackle	6-4	250	1960, 1961-69, 1971	Los Angeles Chargers, San Diego Chargers, Oakland Raiders
Jim Tyrer	Tackle	6-6	274	1961-62, 1963-73, 1974	Dallas Texans, Kansas City Chiefs, Washington Redskins
Ed Budde	Guard	6-5	265	1963-76	Kansas City Chiefs
Billy Shaw	Guard	6-2	258	1961-69	Buffalo Bills
Jim Otto	Center	6-2	248	1960-74	Oakland Raiders
Joe Namath	**Quarterback**	**6-2**	**195**	**1965-76, 1977**	**New York Jets, Los Angeles Rams**
Clem Daniels	Running Back	6-1	220	1960, 1961-67, 1968	Dallas Texans, Oakland Raiders, San Francisco 49ers
Paul Lowe	Running Back	6-0	205	1960, 1961, 1963-68, 1968-69	Los Angeles Chargers, San Diego Chargers, Kansas City Chiefs
George Blanda	**Kicker**	**6-2**	**215**	**1949-58, 1960-66, 1967-75**	**Chicago Bears, Houston Oilers, Oakland Raiders**
DEFENSE					
Jerry Mays	End	6-4	252	1961-62, 1963-70	Dallas Texans, Kansas City Chiefs
Gerry Philbin	End	6-2	245	1964-72, 1973	New York Jets, Philadelphia Eagles
Houston Antwine	Tackle	6-1	270	1961-70, 1971	Boston Patriots, New England Patriots
Tom Sestak	Tackle	6-4	260	1962-68	Buffalo Bills
Bobby Bell	Linebacker	6-4	228	1963-74	Kansas City Chiefs
George Webster	Linebacker	6-4	223	1967-72, 1972-73, 1974-76	Houston Oilers, Pittsburgh Steelers, New England Patriots
Nick Buoniconti	Linebacker	5-11	220	1962-68, 1969-74, 1976	Boston Patriots, Miami Dolphins
Wille Brown	Cornerback	6-1	190	1963-66, 1967-78	Denver Broncos, Oakland Raiders
Dave Grayson	Cornerback	5-10	187	1961-62, 1963-64, 1965-70	Dallas Texans, Kansas City Chiefs, Oakland Raiders
Johnny Robinson	Safety	6-1	205	1960-62, 1963-71	Dallas Texans, Kansas City Chiefs
George Saimes	Safety	5-11	186	1963-69, 1970-72	Buffalo Bills, Denver Broncos
Jerrel Wilson	Punter	6-2	222	1963-77, 1978	Kansas City Chiefs, New England Patriots

Lyle Alzado
Streetfighter

out of the ghetto and into the limelight

A few decades ago, rowdy young American hoodlums from the wrong side of town found that they could fight their way out of the ghetto via the boxing ring. In more modern times, the gridiron is the stage for such feats of social climbing. Lyle Alzado is a perfect example of the bad kid turned good. In fact, so good that, even in retirement, the marauding bearded monster will have a luxurious life and respect.

He rose from being a New York streetfighter to a well-spoken, soft-hearted media star. In the middle, Alzado was one of the roughest-toughest defensive ends that the NFL had seen. What's more, Lyle achieved his celebrity status despite being told on more than one occasion that he was a washed-up no-good. Each time that happened, the big man proved his critics wrong and went on to even better things.

★

Alzado looked fierce, but off the field he was witty and well-spoken.

★

Alzado was brought up in a very tough area of Long Island, New York, where the chances were that gang fights would get him into jail rather than into the NFL. Nevertheless, Lyle made a decision to go to a small South Dakota college to get him out of the rut he was in.

The idea worked. Alzado proved to be quite a scholar, got his degree, and made such an impression on the college team (he was actually the first player ever drafted from it) that he was a fourth-round pick of the Denver Broncos in 1971.

The Broncos at the time were struggling in the depths of the AFC West. There was nothing spectacular about the team and Alzado also struggled to make an impression although he was their sack leader in both '74 and '75.

He relied on a fierce intensity rather than size to pressurize and sack opposing quarterbacks — always his favourite pastime.

At around 250 lb and 6ft 3in, he was never a natural giant of a defensive end, but he had bug-eyed desire and no little cunning amongst his many attributes.

Slowly, the team began to win more than they lost. Alzado was one third of an All-Pro defensive line. He was on the right, Barney Chavous was on the left and Rubin Carter was at nose tackle. The three-man front was something of a rarity in those days and it put extra pressure on Lyle and his two colleagues. They responded magnificently. The Denver defense became the team's trump card. They were known as the 'Orange Crush', but they needed an improved offense to make things happen. In 1977, they got one. Riding a wave of emotion, Denver took their first AFC West title, beat their nemesis Oakland for the conference title and met Dallas in Super Bowl XII.

Alzado was one of the keys to a defense that had continually done the brunt of the work. In the Super Bowl, the offense caved in with four early interceptions and the defense couldn't hold a steady Dallas team. The Broncos lost 27-10.

Their right end, however, was defensive player of the year and made his first Pro Bowl. He was to repeat this post-season appearance in '78.

But the NFL is tough, even on its heroes. In the '79 pre-season, Denver traded Lyle to Cleveland for three draft picks. It seemed like a pretty good deal for Denver — after all, Alzado was 30 years old.

A man with the background of Alzado should never be under-

Alzado bursting through into the backfield as an LA Raider.

estimated, however. He brought that emotion from Denver and used it to help the Cleveland defense gell into a workable unit. By 1980, the Browns were back in the play-offs after an eight-year absence.

In the next season, the team fell apart. Although Alzado led the defense in sacks, he was traded again. This time, he almost came home as he joined the Raiders who were newly ensconced in their Los Angeles stadium. The Raiders had always been masters of football reclamation projects. Alzado was such an item and his larger-than-life personality fitted in just fine with a bunch of mavericks who saw the whole of the world as their enemy.

Again he delighted in proving a team wrong to discard him. In his first year as a Raider in '82, he totalled seven sacks in the strike-shortened season and was named comeback player of the year.

His so-called comeback (to Alzado, it was just a normal career move) was highlighted two years later with a Super Bowl XVIII winners ring after victory over Washington. The Redskins were said to have the best power fullback in the league in John Riggins whose special short-yard gainer was over the left side of his line.

That would put Riggins straight down Alzado's throat. It could be a significant tussle. In fact, Riggins made just 64 yards all night. Alzado had won another battle. And that's just how he saw his life in the trenches — as a man-on-man battle, the sporting equivalent of a knife fight in his home town. He was often in trouble for taking that idea too far and getting into on-the-field brawls.

This varied career ended with a leg injury in 1985 and Alzado had passed the age of 36. By this time, the nation had seen him in a different style. Nearby Hollywood discovered that this bear-of-a-man with his gruff appearance was also well-spoken and witty. Endorsements followed. Adverts on TV came by the bundle. Alzado became the nutty football player who was a real-life teddy bear. When he retired, Lyle appeared on the Johnny Carson Show to tell America he would concentrate on a career in TV and acting.

That's one helluva long way from a gang fight in Brooklyn, but it completed the remarkable story of an athlete with an inner desire to get to the top.

As a defensive end, it's not always just technique that puts your hand in the quarterback's face or your body in the way of a fullback, Alzado didn't lack that technique, but he had a greater ally in the desire to win — it helped take him all the way.

★★★   Lyle Alzado   ★★★

Defensive end. 6ft 3in, 250 lb. Born in Brooklyn, New York, 3 April 1949. Attended Yankton College. 1971-78 Denver Broncos, 1979-81 Cleveland Browns, 1982-85 Los Angeles Raiders.

Sammy Baugh
Slingin' Sammy
his career read like a
Hollywood movie

If Hollywood scriptwriters could have typed out the definitive
football movie story of the 1930s, it could easily have been Sammy
Baugh's real-life experience.

For the man they called Slingin' Sammy wasn't just a game-
breaking passer of the pigskin, he was the first real passer — a true
history-maker. His effect on the game from his first season in 1937
was as dramatic as any feature film plot. That year, as a supposedly-
dumb rookie from the Deep South, Baugh threw the football where
no man had dared to throw it before.

Sammy's arm was special. His pass was true. His spiral was
perfection. Baugh used to practice tossing the ball through a
swinging tyre tied to a tree branch — quite some party piece in the
days when footballs were meant to be carried, not thrown.

Sammy slings another long bomb downfield. In all, he threw for 21,886 yards in sixteen
seasons.

So, when Sammy displayed those skills in the NFL championship game of '37, it came as a surprise to his opponents, the Chicago Bears. The mighty Bears lost 28-21. It was the Redskins first world title and it happened to come in their first year in America's capital (previously the Skins had been based in Boston).

Such a win made Baugh's huge $5,000 signing-on fee seem like the best investment in gridiron history. That was the sort of money that Redskin owner George Preston Marshall had to come up with to stop Baugh slipping into a career as a baseball pitcher — something he did even better than football throwing.

When Baugh entered the sport, the gridiron game was beginning

The classic quarterback pose of the forties: Baugh even played the part in his movies.

to change. In those days, Baugh played as a tailback and always received the ball in a long snap rather than the modern-day style where the QB stands close-up to the centre. So, he was originally expected to run like a tailback, as well as pass like a quarterback. After his first season it was his passing that the Redskins concentrated on.

In fact, the whole of the NFL concentrated on Baugh's development of the passing game. For Washington, the pass became as important (if not more so) than the run — something that was unheard of before he arrived on the scene.

With Baugh at the controls, the Redskins became a team to watch. They began to rattle off winning seasons like clockwork.

In 1940, however, both the QB and his team blotted their copybooks when they lost by the still-record 73-0 to the rampant Chicago Bears — ample compensation for the defeat of '37. Baugh actually had a TD-pass dropped in the end zone when the score was only 7-0. 'Yeah, I suppose it would have made it 73-7,' he commented. But revenge was sweet two years later when Baugh inspired a 14-6 win over the Bears. He threw for one TD and also helped set up the winning score.

There would be two more NFL title games — in 1943 and 45 — but both have unhappy memories for the tall Texan. In the '43 game, Sammy spent the first half watching from the bench — he'd suffered concussion on the opening kick return. He returned in the second half to throw two six-pointers, but the Bears won this one 41-21.

Two years later, Baugh was involved in one of football's craziest moments. It was a freezing, blustery day when the Skins met the Cleveland Rams for the championship. In the first quarter, Washington were up against it. The Rams had them near their own goal-line and Baugh had to drop into his own end zone to try a pass. He was aiming long, but the ball never made it past the goal posts, which in those days were on the goal-line and not the backline. The ball struck the post and fell through the end zone giving a two-point safety to Cleveland. Ironically, Washington lost the game by one point. Needless to say, the rules have now been changed.

Far from winding down his aerial assault on footballing history, Baugh continued reaching passing peaks.

In 1947 (his eleventh pro season), Sammy set records for attempts, completions, yards gained and touchdown passes. A year later he re-wrote three out of four of those marks, missing out on only the touchdown total. But despite his excellence, the team was beginning to slide to the lower ranks. After his sixteenth season (1952), Sammy decided to finish as a footballer.

However, in keeping with his movie-style impact on the sport, Baugh took up a new career — acting. His Texas drawl, rugged good looks and slender figure fitted neatly into a cowboy outfit. Sammy became a B movie star. This unusual but apt turn of events shouldn't detract from a sparkling football playing career. Baugh later tried his hand at coaching (he worked for the AFL New York Titans and Houston Oilers), but had no success.

That ficticious Hollywood script about Baugh would never have needed to stretch to those coaching efforts. There were sixteen NFL seasons in which the gentle man from Texas wrote his own script — that one changed the history of pro football.

★★★ Sammy Baugh ★★★

Quarterback. 6ft 2in, 180 lb. Born in Temple, Texas, 17 March 1914. Attended Texas Christian University. 1937-52 Washington Redskins.

Passing statistics

Year	Attempts	Completions	Percentage passes completed	Yards	Touch-down	Interceptions
1937	171	81	47.4	1,127	7	14
1938	128	63	49.2	853	5	11
1939	96	53	55.2	518	6	9
1940	177	111	62.7	1,367	12	10
1941	193	106	54.9	1,236	10	19
1942	225	132	58.7	1,524	16	11
1943	239	133	55.6	1,754	23	19
1944	146	82	56.2	849	4	8
1945	182	128	70.3	1,669	11	4
1946	161	87	54.0	1,163	8	17
1947	354	210	59.3	2,938	25	15
1948	315	185	58.7	2,599	22	23
1949	255	145	56.9	1,903	18	14
1950	166	90	54.2	1,130	10	11
1951	154	67	43.5	1,104	7	17
1952	33	20	60.6	152	2	1
Totals	**2,995**	**1,693**	**56.5**	**21,886**	**186**	**203**

Rushing: 318 attempts, 324 yards, 1.0 average and 6 touchdowns.

Raymond Berry
The Perfectionist
made himself into a great receiver

Raymond Berry had a philosophy about football. It was a fairly simple, homespun idea which has handed down from his father. Berry believed that he could do something each day that would make him a better player.

He lived by that philosophy as a college player, as a pro player and, later, as a coach. But it was for the thirteen years that he spent as a receiver with the Baltimore Colts that it proved most successful.

All players practise their skills in the gridiron game, but Berry out-practised everybody.

He felt that the more times he caught a football in practice, the more likely he would catch the crucial passes in the game. It worked so well that Berry caught a phenomenal 631 passes which, when he retired in 1967, was the best in the NFL — as was his yardage of 9,275.

It was as a favourite target of the great Colts quarterback Johnny Unitas that Berry made his name. At Southern Methodist University, he'd certainly not looked like a Hall-of-Famer. In three years at SMU, he scored just one touchdown.

It wasn't until the twentieth round of the 1955 draft that the Colts decided to give a chance to the near-sighted, relatively slow (for a receiver, anyway) Berry.

In the event, they were soon impressed by his work ethic, his super-safe hands and his exceptional jumping ability. Actually making the team was quite an achievement after being such a low-round pick, but it wasn't until his third season that Berry began to catch the eye of fans and commentators alike. Significantly, that was the year Unitas began to show his influence.

That 1957 season saw Berry lead the Colts in receptions. He would go on to lead the whole league three times in the following three years.

In 1958, Berry played a leading role as the Colts won their first NFL title in the now-famous overtime win over the New York

Berry's key role in the '59 championship game shouldn't be forgotten.

Giants. As the Colts trailed in that game with time slipping away, Berry caught three key passes in the drive that ended with a game-tying field goal. Then, in the drive that would win Baltimore the game, Berry picked off two more passes to help see the Colts to victory. Raymond's statistics for that game read: twelve catches for 178 yards and one touchdown.

In 1961, he had his best ever season with 75 receptions (although he didn't lead the league), but a series of injuries in the sixties would hamper his performances.

Even so, in 1964 Berry became the NFL's leading receiver. Only the influence of the pass-crazy AFL prevented him sitting on top of the pile for more than eight years.

Injuries reduced his effectiveness by 1967 and that year Berry retired at the age of 34. He took up coaching (first as an assistant at Dallas) but could never expect players to emulate his personal dedication as a Colt.

Berry worked out that he had 88 different moves to outwit

It was the ability to catch anything and everything which made Berry special.

defensive ends. He practised all these moves every single week. He would put himself through extra practice sessions and, once the Colts refused to stay behind any longer, he'd rope in coaches, journalists or even his wife to help out.

He also practised recovering fumbles — yet that was something he prided himself he never did. Not since he lost possession during a college game inside his own 30-yard line. It cost him his place on the team.

During the ten hours per day of football and in his spare time, Berry would do other things to help his game. He kneaded putty between his fingers to strengthen them and kept comprehensive notes on all Colts plays and those of his opponents. His thoroughness didn't stop there. When Berry had trouble with the sun during games on the West coast, he made himself some sun goggles and even wore three different types of contact lens depending on the condition of the game. Even in team warm-ups before matches, he would throw himself about with such abandon that he started the game in a uniform dirtier than some players finished it.

Berry wasn't born with spectacular skills, so he was truly a self-made player. He wa also a self made-coach, not fitting into the normal larger-than-life category, but using his own style, that of a laid-back, fatherly teacher. He took the New England Patriots to their first ever Super Bowl just over a year after he became their head coach.

It was a timely reminder of the devotion that the man had shown as a player.

Those stories about the incredible number of hours he put into the job of being a receiver seemed unbelievable, more so because Berry himself makes light of the statistics which they helped accumulate.

Raymond Berry would have been just a normal football player except for his abnormal work methods. He might have been a relatively unremarkable athlete, but he was definitely a remarkable man.

★★★ Raymond Berry ★★★

End. 6ft 2in, 187 lb. Born in Corpus Christi, Texas, 27 February 1933. Attended Southern Methodist University. 1955-67 Baltimore Colts.

Receiving statistics

Year	Receptions	Yards	Average	Longest	Touchdowns
1955	47	800	17.0	67	6
1956	56	794	14.2	54	9
1957	47	800	17.0	67	6
1958	56	794	14.2	54	9
1959	66	959	14.5	55	14
1960	74	1,298	17.5	70	10
1961	75	837	11.6	44	0
1962	51	687	13.5	37	3
1963	44	703	16.0	64	3
1964	43	663	15.4	46	6
1965	58	739	12.7	40	7
1966	56	786	14.0	40	7
1967	11	167	15.1	41	1
Total	631	9,278	14.7	70	68

Scoring record: 68 touchdowns, 408 points.

George Blanda
The Timeless Wonder

kicking and throwing for more than a quarter of a century

The America of 1949 had Harry Truman as president and the Korean War looming. In football the National Football League was merging with the rogue All America Football Conference and the Chicago Bears drafted clean-cut 6ft 2in George Blanda in the twelfth round as placekicker and third-string quarterback from Kentucky.

Twenty-six years later Gerald Ford was in the White House and the Vietnam War was ending — but in football some things hadn't changed. The Timeless Wonder George Blanda, was still playing. Blanda's is the longest career history known to pro football. He missed one season out of 27, played 340 games, scored 2,002 career

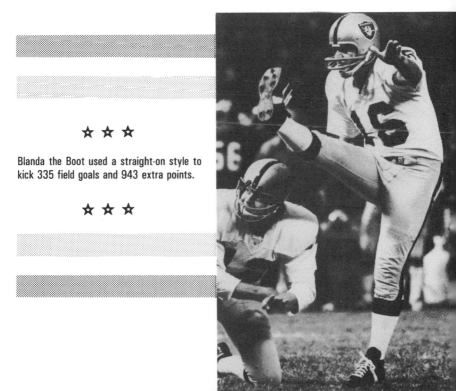

★ ★ ★

Blanda the Boot used a straight-on style to kick 335 field goals and 943 extra points.

★ ★ ★

points, missed only sixteen conversions in 959 attempts, booted 335 field goals and still found time to throw for 26,000 yards and 236 touchdowns. During his younger days he even ran in for nine TDs himself.

To be playing for almost a generation is mind-numbing but to be doing it at such a high performance level and as both placekicker and quarterback is just what makes a football legend. George Blanda began his career slowly with the Bears. He was even traded to Baltimore for a short time in 1951 but returned to Chicago to kick and also start at quarterback. During the early fifties he even went more than five seasons without missing an extra point (156 in a row) such was his kicking skill.

But the Bears enjoyed only moderate success at this time (just one NFL championship game in 1956 which they lost) and Blanda was released in 1959. For a whole season no one picked up his contract and his footballing days could have been over.

A ten-year career would be adequate for most men, but George got a new lease of life when a rival league started. He went to Houston and was better than ever.

In those early pass-happy AFL years Blanda set a record of 36 TD passes in a season and led the Oilers to the first two AFL titles. His seven years in Texas were his most fruitful years as a passer. Blanda led the Oilers to victory in the inaugural AFL championship game versus the Los Angeles Chargers. He threw for 301 yards and three TDs. The wide open spaces of the early AFL games certainly suited his attacking throwing style.

When a new head coach came to Houston in 1966, George was traded again, this time to Oakland. The Raiders already had an outstanding passer in Daryle Lamonica, so George's kicking became more important. In his first year at Oakland, Blanda helped them to a divisional title with 116 points. He also played in Super Bowl II in his first year. In that contest he kicked two extra points but missed a field goal in the 33-14 defeat against Green Bay. But his greatest year was yet to come.

In 1970 he won the NFL Most Valuable Player award (he had already won the same accolade in the AFL in 1961) when he had an incredible sequence of game-winning passes and kicks. He won six consecutive games for the Raiders that year with last-ditch TD throws or field goals. All at the age of 44. Blanda was only stopped from another Super Bowl appearance by three interceptions and a

The chiselled face and grey hair were Blanda's trademark by the end of his career in 1975.

super show by opposing QB Johnny Unitas who led his Baltimore ·
Colts to victory. He had been brought in as a stop-gap kicker at
Oakland — he stayed nine years. But eventually time caught up with
the old master. After the 1975 season when the Raiders had another
new passing star in Ken Stabler and after he missed an
unprecedented (for him, anyway) four extra points, Blanda hung up
his boots for the last time — but only after he turned up at training
camp for the following season!

The gnarled face with its mop of grey hair had seen and won
many battles. Blanda played in eleven championship games but, like
so many great players, won few major team titles (just two). Yet the
man they called 'Old Folks' Blanda acquired enough personal glory
and records never to be forgotten in the sport.

His longevity is unlikely to be beaten and no one can surely play
for more than a quarter century again while also maintaining

Blanda's high standard. Most records are made to be broken. George Blanda's will be the exception to that rule.

★★★ George Blanda ★★★

Quarterback-kicker. 6ft 2in, 215 lb. Born in Youngwood, Pennsylvania, 17 September 1927. Attended University of Kentucky. 1949-58 Chicago Bears, 1950 Baltimore Colts, 1960-66 Houston Oilers, 1967-76 Oakland Raiders.

Kicking statistics

Club	Year	Field goal attempts	Field goals	Extra points	Extra points missed	Points
Chicago	1949-58	201	88	247	3	511
Houston	1960-66	188	91	301	5	574
Oakland	1967-75	249	156	395	8	863
Total		**638**	**355**	**943**	**16**	**1,948**

Note: Blanda's scoring record of 2,002 points also includes nine rushing touchdowns

Passing statistics

Club	Games	Attempts	Completions	Percentage passes completed	Touchdowns	Interceptions	Yards
Chicago	116	998	445	45.0	48	70	5,936
Houston	98	2,784	1,347	50.1	165	189	19,149
Oakland	126	235	119	50.6	23	18	1,835
Total	**340**	**4,007**	**1,911**	**47.7**	**236**	**277**	**26,290**

John Riggins was the kingpin of Washington's Super Bowl season in 1982 with his unstoppable power at fullback (*Paul Spinelli*).

Super scrambler Fran Tarkenton does one of his catch-me-if-you-can routines during Super Bowl XI when his Vikings lost in the big game for the fourth time (*Vernon J Biever*).

Above The inimitable Broadway Joe Namath of the NY Jets became the first quarterback to pass for more than 4,000 yards in a season (*John Biever*).

Right Left-handed Ken Stabler was something of a QB journeyman with a reputation for winning. Here he's in the Houston Oilers colours (*Vernon J Biever*).

Below Larry Csonka suffered severe headaches at the start of his career with Miami because of the amount of punishment his head took. He had to change his running style to stop the pain (*John Biever*).

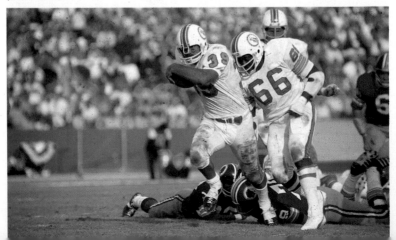

Johnny Unitas could keep his cool in the quarterback pocket as a Boltimore Colt when all around him were losing theirs. It was a talent that made him special (*John Biever*).

The two greatest NFL coaches of all-time, George Halas (left) and Vince Lombardi (right) meet up during a Super Bowl pre-game show (*Vernon J Biever*).

Terry Bradshaw
The Arm of Steel

defeated his opponents and his critics

Luck always plays a part in the shaping of legends. With the Terry Bradshaw story, it began when Pittsburgh won a coin toss which granted them (rather than Chicago) the overall first choice in the NFL draft of 1970. That 'win' would prove to be the most important in Steeler history, a franchise to which on-the-field victories had become an endangered species.

Bradshaw would become the offensive lynchpin for a team that would take the league by storm over the next ten years. Yet his early days at the club showed little indication of what was to come.

Bradshaw's arrival at Pittsburgh in 1970 was one of the major steps in building the great Steeler team of the decade.

Terry had a very strong arm — he was national high school javelin champion.

He arrived at Pittsburgh from relatively-small Lousiana Tech with obvious talent, but it desperately needed honing into a more polished product.

However, there was undoubted power in his right arm. Bradshaw had set a national high school javelin throwing record which proved that the Steelers had an uncut diamond at least. In his rookie season, Terry looked like a confused young man and he played like one, too. It ended with just six touchdowns against 24 interceptions. He needed help. It came in the form of experienced ex-NFL QB campaigner Babe Parelli who took an assistant coaching job. The improvement was sudden. The whole team began to gell and the Steelers almost got themselves a .500 season record, but for a last game 23-14 loss to the LA Rams which included four Bradshaw interceptions.

The emphasis on Bradshaw's arm was then eased in 1972 when runningback Franco Harris was drafted. It lifted some of the pressure and the progress continued as Pittsburgh made the play-offs.

Bradshaw threw a pass (which was to become known as the 'Immaculate Reception') to Harris against Oakland which put them in the AFC title game. There they lost to Miami.

Nevertheless, Bradshaw was beginning to make his team tick. His clashes with coach Chuck Noll had also begun and their love-hate relationship never seemed to resolve itself.

In 1973, for instance, a separated shoulder and the form of stand-in Joe Gilliam added to the player-coach tension, but an 8-1 record in Bradshaw's nine starts that year proved a point.

All the troubles of the past were put aside after the following season. Bradshaw again bowed to the hot arm of Gilliam when the season began, yet he came back to lead the Steelers to a Super Bowl IX victory in his home state of Louisiana.

The learning process was now over as Bradshaw took centre stage. He had the cockiness of a winner and when he spoke, the football world now listened.

They listened even more earnestly after the 1975 season when Pittsburgh once more became Super Bowl champions. Bradshaw was one of the game heroes as he was knocked unconscious completing the game-winning 64-yard TD pass to Lynn Swann.

Wrist and neck injuries plagued Bradshaw a year later and then he broke his wrist in 1977, but showed his tremendous courage by

In this Super Bowl X victory, Bradshaw sets off on a scramble after failing to spot an open receiver.

playing eleven games with a plaster cast. In both years the Steelers made the play-offs, although more Super Bowls eluded them.

Over the next two seasons things changed — they were full of vintage Bradshaw. The QB had come in for more-than-normal beatings from the press who had always portrayed him as a non-starter in the brains stakes.

This myth was further compounded by a now-famous remark made by Super Bowl XIII opponent-to-be Thomas Henderson of Dallas. The brash Cowboy exclaimed that Bradshaw couldn't spell CAT even if he was given the C and A.

Bradshaw had never aspired to suggestions that he was a budding Einstein and, instead, let his playing do the talking. Four touchdown passes and the MVP award said more than any words. Another Super Bowl MVP award (despite three interceptions) followed a year later as Bradshaw and his team completed four world championships in six seasons.

Injuries continued to trouble him right up until a damaged elbow terminated his career possibly a couple of years early in 1983. However, with four Super Bowl rings (he's only kept one for himself and given the rest to his family) there seems little more that he could have achieved. 'One for the thumb' was what Steeler fans called for after Super Bowl XIV, but Bradshaw never got close again.

Towards the end of his career, those critics who had labelled him stupid questioned his motivation and his enthusiasm in the light of some movie appearances. Injury didn't give him a chance to prove them wrong again.

Terry Bradshaw was a truly gifted quarterback. He had one of the most powerful throwing arms in the history of the game and had the vision and bravery to stand in a pocket and use it to superb effect. He called his own plays in the huddle and had to learn to be great because the team he joined were originally far from that.

Bradshaw was lucky to have receivers of the quality of Swann and John Stallworth to fire his passes at during the Steelers era of the seventies which he led.

There was even the original lucky toss of the coin; the toss that enabled the Steelers to draft him in the first place.

But not even Bradshaw's sternest critics could claim that good fortune won him all those games and all those titles. Players as good as he was don't need *that* much luck.

★★★   Terry Bradshaw   ★★★

Quarterback. 6ft 3in, 215 lb. Born in Shreveport, Louisiana, on 2 September 1948. Attended Louisiana Tech. 1970-83 Pittsburgh Steelers.

Passing statistics

Year	Attempts	Com-pletions	Percentage passes completed	Yards	Touch-downs	Inter-ceptions
1970	218	83	38.1	1,410	6	24
1971	373	203	54.4	2,259	13	22
1972	308	147	47.7	1,887	12	12
1973	180	89	49.4	1,183	10	15
1974	148	67	45.3	785	7	8
1975	286	165	57.7	2,055	18	9
1976	192	92	47.9	1,177	10	9
1977	314	162	51.6	2,523	17	19
1978	368	207	56.3	2,915	28	20
1979	472	259	54.9	3,877	26	25
1980	424	218	51.4	3,339	24	22
1981	370	201	54.3	2,887	22	14
1982	240	127	52.9	1,768	17	11
1983	8	5	51.6	77	2	0
Total	3,901	2,025	51.9	27,989	212	210

Jim Brown
Cannonball
probably the greatest powerback of all-time

Cannonball Jim Brown was one of the biggest single sensations in the history of the NFL. He was a graceful, powerful black stallion of a runningback.

He had that exceptional ability to hit a tackler as hard as the tackler tried to hit him. It usually meant that his unfortunate victim bounced off Brown like a rag doll. His concrete-like forearms could push off heavier men and his deceptive loping stride could outrun most of the others. Most people see him as simply the most brilliant runner in football history. The first man past the 10,000-yard barrier; eight NFL rushing titles in a nine-year career and a Pro Bowl

A pose for the camera — good practice for Brown's later acting career.

appearance after each of those nine seasons.

He came into pro football from Syracuse University where he had begun his record-shattering exploits. He also played a fine game of basketball and lacrosse. The young Brown was picked up in the draft of 1957 by Cleveland who were coming to the end of their powerhouse days. Jim Brown was what they needed to pick them up off the floor.

In just the fourth game of his rookie season, Brown galloped for an NFL record 237 yards against the LA Rams. He was named rookie of the year as his team regained their conference title only to lose to Detroit for the NFL championship.

Brown actually spent six months of his first off-season in the army, but came back to record his first 1,000-yard season — it was a mark he would pass in seven of his nine seasons.

Teams were actually spotlighting Jim Brown when they played against his Cleveland side. If you could stop Brown, then the Browns themselves would struggle. To counter, Cleveland came up with a whole new system of offense to give their ace runner the best

Jim Brown in full flight was a fearsome sight for would-be tacklers.

Carving through a defence, Brown would hit
defenders harder than they hit him.

chance of turning up trumps. They adopted an option blocking
pattern which meant their lineman just had to get in the way of
opponents. As long as they could push them off Brown himself, the
sleek runningback could find his own gaps. Opposing linemen were
'guided' in whatever direction they wanted to go because Brown
was good enough to go anywhere *he* wanted to go.

But however hard he seemed to try, Jim's Browns couldn't seem
to put together a championship year. By 1962, Jim was making loud
noises about wanting that title. Rather than lose him, Cleveland's
owner sacked the only coach the team had ever had since they were
formed in 1946, the legendary Paul Brown. Paul Brown (no relation
to his runningback star) had actually given his surname to Cleveland
for their nickname, but he wasn't big enough to stop Jim Brown's
quest for glory.

It came two years later in 1964. Brown himself helped set up the
opening Cleveland TD with a 46-yard run. Although he didn't score
himself, the team turned over the favourite Baltimore Colts for the
championship.

That season and the previous one, when Brown racked up his
highest seasonal yardage total of 1,863, would be the highlights of
his career.

By 1965, Jim had one foot on the road to a movie career. After yet another 1,000-yard season and Pro Bowl appearance, he went off to film *The Dirty Dozen* in England.

Bad weather forced back the schedule and, as the next NFL season was approaching, it was decision time for Brown.

To the despair of every gridiron fan, he chose to stick to films rather than football. There was no doubt that, barring unforseen injury, Jim Brown could have played for at least three more years at the very peak of his profession.

When you consider that Brown never missed a single game due to injury in his nine years at Cleveland, then that career projection was no over-estimation. In fact, he played for much of the 1962 season with a severely strained wrist and still clocked up 996 yards. Perhaps his decision to quit had something to do with the disappointment of the 1965 NFL title game. Against mighty Green Bay, Brown was shackled to just 50 yards and Cleveland lost.

The retirement may also be put down to Brown's ever-growing ego. Hollywood knew how to treat their potential stars and, though Jim was no Olivier, he was good box office, so he was afforded all the film star trappings.

★ ★ ★ ★ ★ ★

Brown played with an anger that had never been seen before on the gridiron.

Football fans might have enjoyed seeing Jim on the big screen, but they'd have preferred him in the big game, for Jim Brown was one of the monumental characters of the sport. He played with an anger and integrity that could be seen in his eyes and felt with his hits. His powerful shoulders and piston-strong legs were his great assets. Hit him with one, two or three men and there was no guarantee that he'd be stopped.

Green Bay Hall of Famer Willie Davis best summed up what it felt like playing against Jim Brown: 'I hit him good and we both went down. It was one of the few times in my life when my whole body was aching. Only pride made me get up.'

Jim Brown was a type of power runningback football hadn't seen before. His career yardage total was an NFL record for more than twenty years and that was about right — Jim Brown probably was twenty years ahead of his time.

★★★ Jim Brown ★★★

Fullback. 6ft 2in, 232 lb. Born in St Simons, Georgia, 17 February 1936. Attended University of Syracuse. 1957-65 Cleveland Browns.

Rushing statistics

Year	Games	Attempts	Yards	Average	Touchdowns
1957	12	202	942	4.7	9
1958	12	257	1,527	5.9	17
1959	12	290	1,329	4.6	14
1960	12	215	1,257	5.8	9
1961	14	305	1,408	4.6	8
1962	14	230	996	4.3	13
1963	14	291	1,863	6.4	12
1964	14	280	1,446	5.2	7
1965	14	289	1,544	5.3	17
Total	118	2,359	12,312	5.2	106

Receiving: 262 catches, 2,499 yards, 9.5 yard average, 20 touchdowns

Passing: 12 attempts, 4 completions, 117 yards, 3 touchdowns

Kick-off returns: 29, 648 yards, 22.3 yard average, 0 touchdowns

Dick Butkus
The Animal
opponents claimed they'd rather face a grizzly bear

Stories about the fearsome middle linebacker Dick Butkus are many and varied. But they all have one thing in common — they prove that the man they called 'The Animal' played football with brutish anger that no one else could match.

Butkus was once charged with biting a referee. An opposing runningback once said of him: 'I pray that I can get up every time Butkus hits me'. The media even gave him extra nicknames to try and classify his ferocity. They called him 'The Enforcer', the 'Maestro of Mayhem', the 'Robot of Destruction'. But it was the tag of 'The Animal' that stuck. He prowled the gridiron like a jungle and not many men messed with Butkus in his nine seasons as the hub of the Chicago Bears defense.

★ ★ ★

Butkus looked the part of the mean, hungry linebacker.

★ ★ ★

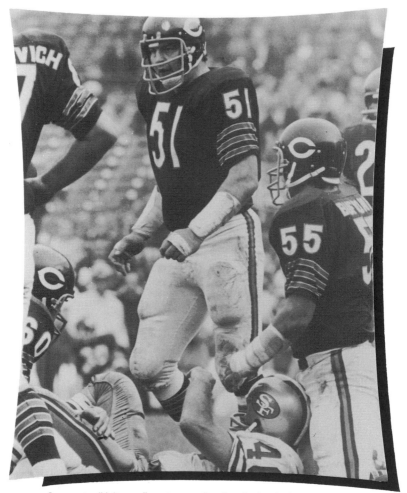

Opponents didn't usually get up easily after Butkus had tackled them.

He'd arrived in the NFL from Illinois University after turning down an astronomical offer from the AFL Denver Broncos. Butkus preferred to stay in his home state rather than go to Denver and took up the Bears $200,000 four-year contract. But Chicago already had fourteen-year veteran Bill George (a Hall of Famer of the future) at middle linebacker so how would Butkus get into the team?

Even George knew the answer to that one: 'The minute that guy walked into camp, I started packing my gear. There was no way he wasn't going to be great.'

Butkus had an immediate impact on the Bears and ended his rookie season of '65 by leading the team in fumble recoveries and pass interceptions. Playing in the pros had finally happened — and in a big way. But it was no accident. Butkus had set his sights on that goal from a very early age. His schools were chosen to give him the best football rather than classroom education while he also spent his summers at training camps.

In those days Butkus played fullback where he understood the art of rushing. This came in more than handy when he developed another art — that of stripping the football from the men in possession. His conversion to linebacker gave better outlet to his fierceness. At 6 ft 3 in and with great speed, Butkus preceded his pro career with outstanding college feats. The Fightin' Illini had a Rose Bowl season helped by Butkus in 1964 when he also finished third in the Heisman Trophy voting.

So it was with that background that Butkus came into the NFL. He was taken in the first round by the Bears along with runningback Gale Sayers in a dream draft for Chicago. 'It's all I can do to figure out where I am supposed to be', was Butkus' first reaction to playing with the big guys. But his determination and commitment was such that he prided himself in never making the same mistake twice.

His individual rating was always high as a Bear. He played in eight straight Pro Bowls in his first eight years and was constantly made all-NFL by the press. Yet his team never had any kind of success. Two winning seasons out of nine was no way for such a player to pass through the NFL ranks. He never played a post-season game.

Nevertheless, the statistics Butkus totted up make impressive reading. He recovered 25 fumbles (an NFL record at the time) and grabbed 22 interceptions. That total of 47 takeaways is still a Bears record despite the Monsters of Midway defense and the current crop of brilliant yardage stoppers.

In among all that hitting, Butkus even returned a few kick-offs, once rushed 28 yards on a fake punt and even more incredibly, he caught two end zone passes for extra points after fumbled snaps had aborted kicking attempts. Such tales just added to the legend.

But the end of Butkus was tinged with sadness and anger of the

wrong sort. He injured his right knee in 1970 but off-season surgery failed to cure the problem. He played in pain for the next two seasons. Finally, in 1973, the pain became too much even for this huge-hearted man. In one game that season against Atlanta, Butkus actually took himself from the field because he was in agony. A few weks later he retired forever.

But that wasn't the end of the story. Butkus filed a lawsuit against the club, charging them with improper handling of his injury. The case was settled out of court but the problems with the right knee haven't been settled — Butkus has those for life. Butkus was told he would never again run, jump or stand for any length of time. He might even need an artificial knee. However, the hurt between man and club has faded with time. Now Butkus even provides colour commentary on the Bears own radio service.

Being part of the great NFL media-go-round isn't the only work that came his way during retirement. The suitably-evil stare got him a few tough guy movie parts and that led to TV appearances on shows ranging from Magnum PI to the Love Boat and Taxi.

There's no bitterness now. 'Few people get to earn a living at what they like to do and there are hazards in any profession. Football is something I was made for. I gave the game all I could for as long as I could,' he said during a recent interview.

His football instinct, strength, leadership, and almost animal-like desire to get the job done meant that what Butkus could give was more than many people could take. As one of his opponents put it: 'I'd sooner go one-on-one with a grizzly bear than Dick Butkus!'

★★★ Dick Butkus ★★★

Linebacker. 6ft 3in, 245 lb. Born in Chicago, Illinois on 9 December 1942. Attended University of Illinois. 1965-73 Chicago Bears.

Interceptions: 22, 166 yards, 7.5 yard average, 0 touchdowns.
Kick-off returns: 12, 120 yards, 10.0 yard average, 0 touchdowns.

In nine seasons with the Chicago Bears, Butkus recovered an astonishing 25 fumbles.

Earl (Dutch) Clark
The Earl of the Gridiron
one of the first kings of the gridiron game

Dutch Clark had anything but your typical career way back in the days of leather football helmets. He was a stand-out in college who was recognised an an All-American in 1929, yet didn't step foot on a professional field until 1931.

Clark attended the small Colorado College where he was brilliant both in the classroom and on the field. His genius for quick-thinking provided for innumerable great moments.

Trailing the University of Denver 2-0 late in a big game, Clark tried one of his infamous dropkicks for a 33-yard field goal which the referee signalled no good. 'Why not?' Clark inquired. 'Because it was wide. The ball went directly over the east goal post,' the official explained. 'Then it is good,' Clark answered and quickly produced a rule book to prove he was right. Clark helped pace Colorado College for four seasons in this manner. His all-round talents won that Denver game but it was his knowledge of the game that put him in the Pro Hall of Fame.

American football in the 1930s wasn't anything like what we see today. Teams were being born, salaries were pitiful and conditions were brutal. For these reasons players like Clark shined brighter than ever.

Clark (whose given name was Earl) joined his first pro club, the Portsmouth Spartans, for the 1931 season. The Spartans, formed just one year earlier in Portsmouth, Ohio, were having their share of financial problems. Little was recorded about those initial years in Clark's career. There were no statistics kept for the 1931 season when the Spartans finished second to Green Bay. In '32 they were third and then Clark gave up football for a year to become head coach at a small Rocky Mountain school, the Colorado School of Mines because he could earn more money there than playing pro football.

He returned to pro football in 1934 but, by that time, the Portsmouth Spartans had become the Detroit Lions. The 'new' club

Clark was an all-round scoring threat and the last of the NFL dropkickers.

were experiencing all the 'old' problems — no money, low crowds, different identity.

When he returned, Clark was said by some to be one of the slowest players on the team. But he was no quitter. He worked hard alongside his teammates and provided a stability that the entire team began to depend on. It became so apparent that he was a key figure, that he was assigned a coaching position on the team but continued to play as well. Throughout his career, he played with another handicap, that of severely-limited vision in one eye.

But neither his slowness nor his bad sight could prevent him from becoming one of the greatest players football has ever seen. His determination goes beyond his average-looking statistics and his ability was the major reason behind the Lions winning the NFL title in 1935.

For the five years after Clark returned to pro football, he was a crucial factor in the Detroit's infantry attack. Their ground game was so intense that the 2,885 yards the Lions accumulated in 1936

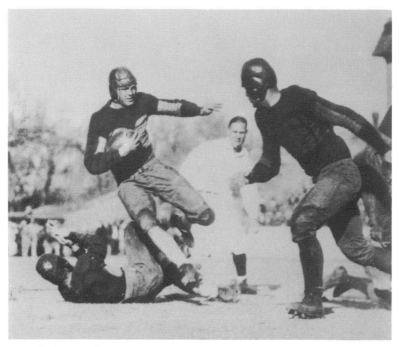
In the days of the leather helmet, Dutch Clark was a major ground gainer.

was a team rushing record in the NFL for years. Detroit, in fact, has led the league in rushing in only three season, 1936, 1937 and 1938 — Clark was at the helm of the attack in all three years. He called the plays and was named an all-NFL quarterback six of his seven seasons but he also played tailback much of the time. Clark was the true triple-threat of the Lions.

In 1936 he finished third in rushing with 628 yards. He led the Lions in passing and completed 53.5 per cent in a year when the overall league completion average was just 36.5 per cent. Clark also was one of the last great dropkickers, an art now strictly reserved for the history books. He led the league in scoring and was Detroit's conversion and field goal specialist.

Clark had the talent of always being in the right place at the right time. His teammates will swear that no one could follow his blockers as well as Clark. It was said that on a 40-yard scoring scamper, Clark might well cover 100 yards following his blockers back and forth across the field. 'Dutch is like a rabbit in a brush heap,' said coach

Potsy Clark (no relation). 'When he gets into the secondary, he has no plan, just instinct'.

This was no typical career at all. Clark was capable of doing it all. He battled indecision and pulled through with flying colours. In his short playing life, Clark was prodigious in several different roles. From player to coach and back to player he became the heart of football in the thirties.

Earl (Dutch) Clark has become one of the kings of football past. His was an extra-ordinary career because he was an extra-ordinary man. His time with football was small, but his effect was everlasting.

★★★   Earl (Dutch) Clark   ★★★

Quarterback. 6ft 0in, 185 lb. Born in Fowler, Colorado, 11 October 1906. Died 5 August 1978. Attended Colorado College. 1931-32 Portsmouth Spartans, 1934-38 Detroit Lions.

Rushing statistics

Year		Attempts	Yards	Average	Touchdowns
+ 1931	No Statistics				
+ 1932		111	461	4.2	2
1933	Did Not Play				
● 1934		123	763	6.2	6
● 1935		120	412	3.4	4
● 1936		123	628	5.1	6
● 1937		96	468	4.9	5
● 1938		7	25	3.6	0
Total		**457**	**2,757**	**3.9**	**23**

+ with Portsmouth Spartans
● with Detroit Lions

Larry Csonka
Zonk
a runningback with the impact of a truck

Larry Csonka was a human runaway truck. Hand him the football and he seemed able to crash through an army of would-be tacklers by using mere brute force.

His name — pronounced 'Zonka' with the C silent — even sounds like the explosive noise of this 230 lb frame of iron smashing into a line of opponents.

Csonka was a fullback's fullback. If ever a ball carrier dipped his shoulder lower or rammed his head harder into more linebackers, then no one has ever found him. His kamikaze courage allowed him to bludgeon defensive lines into submission rather than trick his way past them with fancy footwork.

Csonka might have won fame as a Dolphin, but his style of play couldn't be more dislike this most graceful of sea creatures. This particular Dolphin was a creature of raw, unrefined power. This granite-tough fullback was the epitome of the record-setting Miami team of the early seventies. He played a major role in the perfect 17-0 season of 1972 and was Dolphin coach, Don Shula's archetypal player — nothing fancy, just dedicated and hard-working.

Csonka was Miami's first pick in the draft of '68 and was joined by his future running partner Jim Kiick. Coach Shula was building up a fine pool of talent and Csonka (who had won All-America honours at the University of Syracuse) was put to work as the offensive battering ram.

The Dolphin franchise was only two years old and just winning a handful of games required exceptional determination.

Csonka was one of the leaders in effort. In fact, his head-ramming style left him with continual headaches during his early seasons at Miami. It would mean a change in style (more use of his meaty forearms and tree-strong thighs) but no one questioned his continual effort.

The hard work began to pay off in 1970 when the Dolphins made the post-season action for the first time. However, Csonka and the

The muscular forearms protecting the pigskin and The Zonk was on the run.

whole team were slowed by the muddy Oakland pitch and they lost to the Raiders 21-14.

The improvement continued the next season as Zonk became the club's first-ever 1,000-yard rusher. The press christened him and Kiick 'Butch Cassidy and the Sundance Kid'. Kiick's job was primarily to block for Csonka who promptly ran over people.

It was enough for the team to make Super Bowl V against Dallas. However, it wasn't a happy day for Zonk or the Dolphins. On only Miami's second possession, Csonka fumbled. The Cowboys recovered and the drive brought them a field goal. The mistake set the tone of the game and Dallas won easily 24-3. Zonk gained only 40 yards. The Dolphins had clearly lacked big-match experience.

Now they had it, they put it to the ultimate use. In 1972, Miami were unbeatable. Csonka had another 1,000-yard year and Miami won all fourteen regular season games. They made the Super Bowl

and the inevitable happened with victory over Washington. Csonka led the charge with 112 yards on just fifteen carries.

But the Zonk's most memorable individual moment came in the following season when the Dolphins repeated as Super Bowl champions.

For six seasons, Miami's running game was in the 'three-yards-and-a-cloud-of-dust' style with Csonka the man most often on the bottom of the pile when the officials came to judge the next gain. It was a bruising way to earn a living, yet it had its rewards. The greatest of those came in Super Bowl VIII. Zonk ground out 145 yards and ran in two TDs. The Dolphins won again and Csonka got the MVP award.

However, at the very height of his NFL fame, Zonk chose a fresh challenge in a new league. He and several other Dolphins had shown signs of disenchantment before the Super Bowl. The Dolphin adventure had lost its edge of excitement. Csonka, Kiick and Miami wide receiver Paul Warfield were signed up for $3.3 million to the new World Football League. They played out their Miami contracts in 1974, but the sparkle had gone.

☆ ☆ ☆ ☆ ☆ ☆ ☆ ☆ ☆　　　　☆ ☆

Right Csonka's career spanned three teams, two leagues and 1,891 yards.

☆

Left Here against Minnesota in Super Bowl XIII, Csonka is on his way to 145 yards and the MVP award.

☆ ☆ ☆ ☆ ☆ ☆ ☆ ☆ ☆　　　　☆ ☆

The next season, the three set off to join the WFL. It turned out to be a disasterous move. Csonka, playing for Memphis Southmen, tore a muscle in his abdomen after only a couple of games. Their star attraction was out and it was no surprise when the team and the league folded before the season was over.

Csonka's career was in danger of being buried, but the New York Giants signed him on a reported $1 million contract.

The Giants were struggling at the time and Csonka's knees were in need of surgery. He missed much of the season. It was an unhappy time for Zonk who rarely got a starting fullback job and was only wheeled out regularly on short-yardage situations.

There was more than a little sentiment involved in his return to Miami in 1979. Nevertheless, Csonka still had class as was proved in a three-TD show against Chicago. At 33, and after his team lost in that season's play-offs to Pittsburgh (Csonka managed to score one TD), Zonk retired.

Later, he would link up with another rival league to the NFL, the United States Football League, as general manager of the Jacksonville Bulls. But it was a bull on the field that the fans remember Zonk. And many cringe at the memory of the bone-jarring human battering ram dipping his shoulder for another clash of flesh.

★★★　Larry Csonka　★★★

Runningback. 6ft 3in, 230 lb. Born in Stow, Ohio, 25 December 1946. Attended Syracuse University. 1968-74 and 1979 Miami Dolphins. 1975 Memphis Southmen. 1976-79 New York Giants.

Rushing statistics

Year	Attempts	Yards	Average	Touchdowns
+ 1968	138	540	3.9	6
+ 1969	131	566	4.3	2
+ 1970	193	874	4.5	6
+ 1971	195	1051	5.4	7
+ 1972	213	1117	5.2	6
+ 1973	219	1003	4.6	5
+ 1974	197	749	3.8	9
● 1975	Statistics Unavailable			
* 1976	160	569	3.6	4
* 1977	134	464	3.5	1
* 1978	91	311	3.4	6
+ 1979	220	837	3.8	9
Total	**1,891**	**8,081**	**4.3**	**64**

+ with Miami Dolphins
● with Memphis Southmen
* with New York Giants

Art Donovan
Fatso
the cornerstone of a
magnificent team

Many fans believe that most football games are decided from the glamour positions in the offensive backfield. Many players believe that most football games are decided in the trenches, in that man-to-man combat between the opposing linemen.

Back in the fifties, the players' view was, perhaps, never more true. At that time the gridiron game hadn't taken on the appearance of a battle between two multi-million dollar corporations. It was still a muddy muscular grappling match between two sets of gladiators who hated to lose, but hated their opponents more.

Art Donovan played in the game throughout the decade. He was a bull-necked roly-poly man who had the subtlety of a dinosaur, but it didn't matter. He had a snail's speed, but it didn't matter. What he had was a relentless power to bear down on the man opposite him, go straight at him and just knock him on his butt, plain and simple. That was the name of the game in Donovan's day and he took delight in making the most of what he had. It won him a spot on one of pro football's greatest teams and, hence, some great days.

The position of defensive tackle required a slugger's mentality in those days and Donovan had the perfect background. His grandfather had been a middleweight boxing champion and his father a top-rated boxing referee. Coming from the hard-nosed Bronx area of New York, Donovan needed to be tough, but he chose football rather than boxing to use that quality.

He started off at America's most revered football academy, Notre Dame, in 1942, but then the Second World War got in the way.

Donovan spent four years in the Marines. When he returned home, he went to Boston College to complete his schooling and prepare for a shot at pro football. Unfortunately he didn't get an auspicious start.

The Baltimore Colts drafted him, but the franchise folded after a 1-11 year in 1950. Donovan got on the New York Yanks team a year later and then the Dallas Texans in '52. However, before the

A helmet used to prevent opponents from seeing Donovan's angry face, but it didn't prevent him from hitting them.

following season, the Texans' franchise was transferred back to Baltimore. The golden years were not far away. Donovan's reputation had been allowed to grow despite playing on some awful teams. He was considered one of the few assets inherited from the Dallas franchise.

His ability to bludgeon his way to the passer or use his 265 lb, 6ft-3in bulk to shore up the middle of the line against the rush got him All-Pro status in 1954. He would achieve this standard through until 1957 and play in five Pro Bowls. The Colts would have few worries about the middle of their defensive line.

When Weeb Ewbank became head coach in '54, the whole team began a surge to the top. Ewbank would have a great influence on

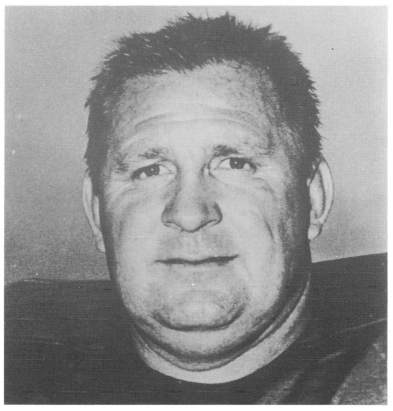

Donovan lived happily with the nickname of 'Fatso' throughout his career.

Donovan as well as the rest of the Colts. While Art led the defense, the coach got the jewel he needed on offense when Johnny Unitas began to show his influence at quarterback.

But 1958 was the year that Donovan and his teammates would particularly remember. The Donovan-inspired defense played to form, especially on two shut-out victories against Green Bay and Chicago. In the NFL championship game against the New York Giants, history would be made: the first title game decided in overtime — and it was in front of a huge TV audience. It would be called the greatest game in pro football and is remembered for Alan Ameche's winning touchdown after a Unitas-led drive. Not many recall that the Colts defense held the Giants on the first overtime possession. A possession that gave the Colts offense the ball and helped set up the win. Donovan remembers.

In the following year's championship game, a Colts-Giants re-match was lined up. The early exchanges were defense-dominated. The Colts defense never caved in and Baltimore won again. Donovan had now helped win two championships. But his huge frame (he claimed never to train) had taken a heavy battering and he survived only two more seasons.

His contribution to the Colts titles of the fifties was quickly rewarded. Shortly after his retirement (Coach Ewbank persuaded him to quit at the top), Donovan's no 70 shirt was retired. There were rumours before the '63 season that he might make a comeback when new coach Don Shula took over from Ewbank, but Donovan was too close to 40 years old and sensibly declined.

However, another honour was soon bestowed on him. In 1968, Donovan was enshrined into the Pro Football Hall of Fame — the first Colt in the history of the club. Defensive players deserve more honours like that. The players realize the power that a big-play defense can give a team, how whole squads can be moved by men who play the game where it's toughest, by men like Art Donovan.

★★★ Art Donovan ★★★

Defensive tackle. 6ft 3in, 265 lb. Born in Bronx, New York, 5 June 1925. Attended Boston College. 1950 Baltimore Colts, 1951 New York Yanks, 1952 Dallas Texans, 1953-61 Baltimore Colts.

Otto Graham
Otto the Great
still ranked at the top thirty years after he retired

In every truly great team there are a cluster of star players, the core of the side, the men that make the big plays. But how much influence does one man have on a great team? Can he single-handedly hoist them to the top of the pile? Otto Graham did at Cleveland. And how do we know? Well, the story is a simple one.

It started when Cleveland's coach, the legendary Paul Brown (the club took his surname as their nickname in his honour), chose Graham to lead his club in the newly-formed league, the All America Football Conference.

Brown had seen his prospective protégé at Northwestern University where he specialized as a single-wing tailback in run-pass options. The Cleveland coach converted the young collegian into a T-formation QB with the emphasis on the pass. The conversion was painless for Graham but it certainly hurt the rest of the AAFC teams. The Brown's opening game was a 44-0 shellacking of the Miami Seahawks — and that was just the beginning.

The first AAFC title (1946) went to Cleveland. The second also went there . . . so did the third . . . and the fourth.

Graham mobilized the troops on the field with such panache and style that his and the team's brilliance were the major downfall of the entire league. The Browns were just too good to make the AAFC a success.

So in 1950 the AAFC merged with the NFL. The experts had long been debating how good the Cleveland boys really were. Surely they would be crushed by the mighty teams of the NFL? If they thought that, then they were to be proved wrong.

In the NFL the Browns rocketed to new heights with Graham as the pilot. They were champions in that first season and Otto himself capped the year with a four-TD performance in the title game.

The NFL felt the power of Graham's arm and rushing for another four seasons as the Browns reached the championship game each year. Unfortunately they only won one.

Above Graham stood at the top of the quarterback ratings list for more than thirty years.

Right The AAFC was not supposed to have the talent of the NFL, but Graham's team took the old league by storm.

Perhaps Graham's best year of all was 1952 when he led the NFL in all the major passing departments — attempts, completions, yardage and touchdowns. Only injuries to key players stopped a rampant Browns in that year's championship game against Detroit. That one title in four attempts came in 1954 (Graham threw two TDs and ran for three more) and afterwards Otto said he would retire.

Surely great players like tackle Lou Groza, end Dante Lavelli and fullback Marion Motley would carry the Browns onto further triumphs? Such optimism in the absence of Graham proved unfounded.

In the 1955 pre-season the Browns collapsed. Graham was brought back for one more year. He responded by reaching his tenth

championship game in a ten year career. He ran for two TDs, passed for two more and the Browns beat LA Rams 38-14.

The Browns have never been the same since. The club has been good in the post-Graham years, but never great. The coolness and deftness of touch which Otto Graham brought to the Cleveland side at the time was its cornerstone.

The man from Waukegan, Illinois, was so good that he still stands at no 2 in the all-time passing ratings. He was top of that list for more than thirty years. Otto Graham had the talent to be the most exceptional player in one of pro football's most exceptional teams.

★★★   Otto Graham   ★★★

Quarterback. 6ft 1in, 195 lb. Born in Waukegan, Illinois, 6 December 1921. Attended Northwestern University. 1946-55 Cleveland Browns.

Passing statistics

Year	Attempts	Completions	Yards	Interceptions	Touchdowns
1946	174	95	1,834	5	17
1947	269	163	2,753	11	25
1948	333	173	2,713	15	25
1949	285	161	2,785	10	19
1950	253	137	1,943	20	14
1951	265	147	2,205	16	17
1952	364	181	2,816	24	20
1953	258	167	2,722	9	11
1954	240	142	2,092	17	11
1955	185	98	1,721	8	15
Total	**1,565**	**872**	**23,584**	**94**	**88**

Rushing: 306 attempts, 682 yards, 2.2 yard average, 33 touchdowns.

No other quarterback in history has led his team to four Super Bowl wins — Terry Bradshaw has with Pittsburgh (*Vernon J Biever*).

Bart Starr led the Green Bay Packers to one of the most dominant periods in NFL football. He also won himself the first two Super Bowl MVP awards (*Vernon J Biever*).

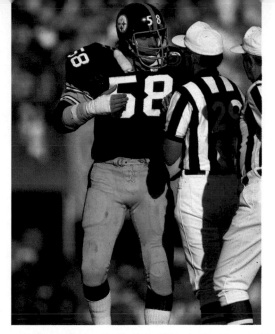

Above When Jack Lambert arrived at Pittsburgh in 1974, the Steel Curtain defense began an unequalled reign of power (*Vernon J Biever*).

Left Roger Staubach never gave up. He had a reputation for winning games that looked like lost causes — something the Dallas fans adored (*Vernon J Biever*).

Below Ten high-pressure years as head coach of the Oakland Raiders saw John Madden take the team to its first Super Bowl win (*Vernon J Biever*).

Bob Lilly was the first man ever drafted by the Dallas Cowboys and came to epitomize the franchise (*Vernon J Biever*).

Jan Stenerud (here kicking for Kansas City Chiefs in Super Bowl IV) had a career spanning a remarkable nineteen top class seasons (*Vernon J Biever*).

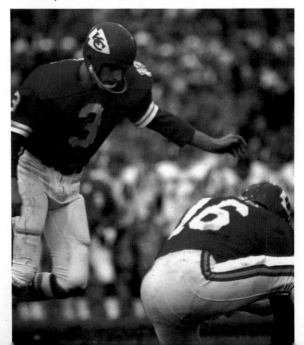

Red Grange
Galloping Ghost
football's first millionaire

Can one man's influence at a certain point in time change history?
Yes, of course it can, but has it ever happened in the history of
football? Yes, of course it has, and the man who did it was Harold
'Red' Grange.

Football experts eulogized about Grange when he was a supreme
all-round talent at the University of Illinois. College football in the
1920s held Grange on high as its hero. The very mention of his name
would bring a look of joy to the face of any football fan in the nation.
He ran with the silky style of a cheetah in the open field and shot
through the merest chink of light between his blocking linemen like
a human drag-racer.

But what would Grange do with all that ability after his three years
of college football, each of which was marked by a 1,000-yard

When Grange decided to turn pro,
the future of the NFL was virtually
assured.

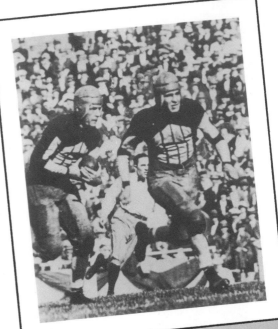

Left 'The Galloping Ghost' they called him. Grange (with the ball) here begins a 95-yard run for the first of his four-touchdowns-in-twelve-minutes performance for Illinois.

Right Grange's reputation was built with the University of Illinois. Here he holds his famous no 77 shirt after his final college game.

rushing total? Some said he would be a butcher. His father and his college coach didn't like the idea of Red turning pro. Nothing was certain until a movie theatre manager and promoter Charles C Pyle decided he wanted to become Red Grange's manager.

The young collegian was sitting in one of Pyle's movie houses when an usher took him to the boss's office. Virtually the first words Pyle said to Red were: 'How would you like to make one hundred thousand dollars? Maybe even a million?' It was an offer that Grange couldn't refuse. The shrewd C.C. Pyle (his business dealings won him the nickname 'Cash and Carry') had agreed to deliver Grange to Chicago Bears owner George Halas in time for the end of the 1925 season.

Pyle's plans for his young charge didn't end there. The entrepreneur arranged a barnstorming end-of-season tour for Grange and the Bears which would mean nineteen games in 47 days. Grange's reputation went before him and 400,000 people paid to see him run. It was an unprecedented feat of courage and durability on the part of both Red and his teammates.

The tour went from coast to coast and, by its end, the future of pro football was secure. One man's decision to unashamedly play football for money had made the difference between the pro game slowly going out of business and it growing into the most popular and profitable sport in America. After the success of the tour, the Pyle/Grange partnership asked for a one-third ownership of the Bears if the two parties were to stay together, Halas refused, so Pyle started his own team and his own league instead with Grange the star.

The American Football League lasted only the one season of 1926 and was a financial disaster. Grange's New York Yankees team was accepted into the NFL a year later and were looking good in their first season when disaster struck. The Yankees were playing Grange's former club, the Chicago Bears, when a tackler fell on Red's right leg. Severely torn tendons were diagnosed and this great player hobbled on crutches for months.

He missed some games, but came back to play too early after the injury. Grange later admitted that the decision to return too quickly cost him much of his flair. Red missed the entire '28 season, but Halas persuaded him to try a comeback with the Bears a year later. The knee injury curtailed those famous dodging, weaving runs, so Grange concentrated on defense. It was hardly surprising that a man of such sporting flair adapted perfectly to his new role. He still carried the ball on offense occasionally, but only as a straight-ahead gainer.

The Bears won two NFL titles with Grange back in their ranks and he finally retired after an exhibition game in January 1935 at the age of 32. Red was assistant coach at Chicago for three more seasons and watched pro football flourish from the sidelines. At the height of his fame, Grange was a national idol. As a hard-up student and college hero he had delivered ice blocks and every housewife on his route dressed in her finery to greet him.

The athlete who delivered ice also went on to make movies in Hollywood during the off-season. He was photographed with flappers, featured on newspaper front pages as well as in their gossip columns, met presidents, toured in a vaudeville show, but it never detracted from his ability to run with a football.

In one game for University of Illinois, Grange scored four touchdowns in twelve minutes with runs of 95, 67, 56 and 46 yards. Later in the game. he threw for another TD and ran for yet another.

Pro football was still an unsteady child when he joined it. His influence guided it confidently towards adulthood. It was done on personality (his flame-red hair and constant smile were his trademarks), but especially on ability. Tributes were paid to his skills many times. However, none was more apt than the poem written by a New York newspaper columnist. It gave Grange his 'Galloping Ghost' nickname and the opening verse went like this:

There are two shapes now moving,
Two ghosts that drift and glide,
And which of them to tackle each rival must decide,
The shift with spectral swiftness across the swarded range,
And one of them's a shadow,
And one of them is Grange.

★★★   Red Grange   ★★★

Halfback. 6ft 0in, 185 lb. Born in Forksville, Pennsylvania, 13 June 1903. Attended Illinois University. 1925 Chicago Bears, 1926 New York Yankees (AFL), 1927 New York Yankees, 1929-34 Chicago Bears.

George Halas
Papa Bear
the father of pro football

They called him 'Papa Bear'. They called him the Father of Pro Football. They called him the game's greatest innovator, its biggest personality, its heart and soul. George Halas was all these things and more to the National Football League which he helped to launch, which he nurtured through the bad times and whose teams he conquered as both player and coach.

From the age of 25 when the NFL was born in a car showroom in Canton, Ohio, to the day he died in the autumn of 1983, Halas' name was synonymous with football. He gave his life to the NFL and his beloved Chicago Bears and the sport gave him some of the greatest moments of his life.

Halas actually played in the league for eleven years. He was only 180 lb, but he played end and threw a mean block. His football career only began after a period with the famous New York Yankees baseball club. It's ironic that a future legend of football was replaced at the Yankees by a future legend of baseball, Babe Ruth.

So, it was to be football for George who had played in the Rose Bowl in 1919, earning the MVP award.

In 1920, Halas was employed by a starch firm boss to run a team known as the Staley Starchmakers. Within two years, Halas gained control of the club and moved it to Chicago. Those were the days when a small band of pro footballers battled against an uninterested nation, too few financial backers and, finally, themselves. They were the pioneers who laid the bedrock for football. Halas was a huge part of all that was good about the game, especially in its formative years.

He would set up the college draft system to equalize the teams, he suggested larger playing squads, he would later champion the idea of shared television revenue, and those were just his off-the-field ideas. As a coach, Halas gave to football a formation which would leave a more lasting impression than any other. The Halas Formation (as it was called by his players) was the 'T' formation with

a man in motion. The 'T' won the Bears the 1940 championship by a score of 73-0 against Washington. That's one mark that will never be beaten.

Halas said he didn't actually invent the formation, but discovered its absolute effectiveness. He was the master of getting the most out of such things, out of his players as well.

Nothing escaped the eye of Halas in his quest for improving the game, but more particularly, the chance of his Bears winning.

He was the first to place a coach high up in the stadium to watch the pattern of play (now called 'the spy in the sky'), he outlawed the rule that only allowed a pass to be thrown within five yards of the line of scrimmage (coincidentally just after one of his own players had won a championship by breaking this rule) and he brought the hashmarks into the centre of the field — a development which opened up the game.

The list of accomplishments seems endless. Yet, it's probably as a championship-winning coach that he might have wanted to be remembered most. Halas coached the Bears for forty years, in four ten-year periods. He won a peerless 326 games out of 506 — that's

☆ ☆ ☆ ☆ ☆

Left Halas coached for forty years with the Bears in four ten-year periods and won a whole bundle of titles.

☆

Right As an offensive end, Halas played for ten years in the pros.

☆ ☆ ☆ ☆ ☆

Papa Bear was always one of the NFL's leading lights. Here he sits with league commissioner Pete Rozelle at a Hall of Fame game.

virtually two out of every three. It's another record that may never be beaten. There were six NFL titles during his tenure. The first was in 1921 when the team were still called the Chicago Staleys and his last was in 1963.

It was the winning that Halas enjoyed most. He brought the best players to Chicago. There was Red Grange, a national college football hero, who Halas used on a twelve-games-in-nineteen days promotional tour that first sparked America's interest in the pro game.

There was Bronko Nagurski, his 1940s squad who won the name of the 'Monsters of Midway', there was Dick Butkus and Gayle Sayers in the sixties, and, if all else failed, there was Halas' indomitable spirit. Who else but Halas would trip up an opposing player who was running for a touchdown — only a crime when you realize Halas was a coach on the sidelines for that game? He put radio receivers in players' helmets (later outlawed), sent spies disguised as painters to study future opponents at their training grounds and once even employed a lip-reader to watch the lips of rival quarterbacks in the huddle during a game.

Halas lived for football and his Bears. He breathed life into the whole sport because of his desire for close competition among the teams. Only age dulled his direct influence with the team. He ended his coaching days in 1967, but never gave up his ownership of Chicago or his backroom work.

Even in death, Halas still seemed to have a hand in team affairs. The Bears hadn't won a championship since 1963 when Halas appointed one of his former players, Mika Ditka, as head coach in '82.

'You'll take us to the Super Bowl in three years', said Halas. Ditka did it in four and won handsomely. Somehow, although Papa Bear died two years earlier, that team was still Halas' Bears.

★★★ George Halas ★★★

End. Coach. Team owner. Born in Chicago, Illinois, 2 February 1895. Attended Illinois University. 1920 Decatur Staleys, 1921 Chicago Staleys, 1922-29 Chicago Bears; coach 1933-42, 1946-55, 1958-67 Chicago Bears. Chairman of the Board of the Bears.

Coaching record

Year	Record	Year	Record	Year	Record
1920	10-1-1	1937	9-1-1	1954	8-4-0
1921*	10-1-1	1938	6-5-0	1955	8-4-0
1922	9-3-0	1939	8-3-0	1956-57	did not coach
1923	9-2-1	1940*	8-3-0	1958	8-4-0
1924	6-1-4	1941*	10-1-0	1959	8-4-0
1925	9-5-3	1942	11-0-0	1960	5-6-1
1926	12-1-3	1943-45	did not coach	1961	8-6-0
1927	9-3-2	1946*	8-2-1	1962	9-5-0
1928	7-5-1	1947	8-4-0	1963*	11-1-2
1929	4-8-2	1948	10-2-0	1964	5-9-0
1930-32	did not coach	1949	9-3-0	1965	9-5-0
1933*	10-2-1	1950	9-3-0	1966	5-7-2
1934	13-0-0	1951	7-5-0	1967	7-6-1
1935	6-4-2	1952	5-7-0	Total	326-150-30
1936	9-3-0	1953	3-8-1		

*Championship seasons
Note: regular season games only

Franco Harris
Italian Stallion
kept one step ahead of everyone, including his critics

'When the going gets tough, the tough get going'. That saying is as true of Franco Harris as it is of any ball carrier in the history of football. When the great Pittsburgh Steelers team of the seventies needed sure yardage, they invariably turned to this dusky, half-black, half-Italian crackerjack runningback.

It's no coincidence that the Steelers reached their first-ever title game in Harris's rookie season of 1972.

From that point on, Harris and Pittsburgh were destined for the record books. He became only the third man past the 10,000-yard barrier. He was a Pro Bowler for nine straight seasons, 1972-80. His mark of six consecutive 1,000-yd rushing seasons was a long-time record in the league while he also held or shared 23 others at one time.

★

Franco's Italian Army was the title given to Harris's huge following among fans at Pittsburgh.

★

Perhaps his only regrettable quality (for the sake of his own reputation, anyway) was that of honesty. Harris actually admitted to feeling fear on the field. Franco would step out of bounds on occasions when he felt he'd got all the yards he was going to get and to avoid a gratuitous hit for a man-hungry linebacker. Some people said this was common sense prevailing while others claimed it wasn't in the true spirit of the game.

Whatever the rights and wrongs, such discretion kept Harris's body intact for thirteen seasons and shouldn't detract from his value to the sport. His very first season brought Harris to the attention of the entire football world. He had rushed for over 1,000 yards in that rookie year but the Steelers' miracle season looked like ending in the opening play-off match against Oakland.

Pittsburgh were 7-6 behind when Bradshaw tried a desperate pass play on fourth down with just 22 seconds of the match remaining. The pass was aimed at Frenchy Fuqua but was deflected by Oakland linebacker Jack Tatum. The deflected ball fell into the path of Harris who scooped it up off his shoe laces and ran 42 yards for the winning TD. The play became one of the most famous in NFL history and was called the 'Immaculate Reception'.

That one touchdown by Harris began the great Steeler years which would bring the club four Super Bowl titles. Those seasons of success meant plenty of tough games for Franco and he always seemed to perform with extra-special fire in them.

He got the ultimate reward in just his third season. He began it sluggishly and then missed two games through injury. The sleeping giant then awoke to crush opponent after opponent to take Pittsburgh to Super Bowl XIX. There was no let-up in the game itself despite Franco suffering a bad cold. He blasted Minnesota for 158 yards on 34 carries and one TD. His yardage total was a then Super Bowl record and it won him the MVP trophy.

The following season brought Harris the best yardage total of his career; 1,246. The Steeler offense relied on those yards to return to the Super Bowl where they beat Dallas. Harris had 27 carries for 82 yards.

As Pittsburgh went for a hat-trick of titles, Harris was again in the thick of things. Franco racked up 132 yards in a play-off game against Baltimore in just over two quarters, but then suffered severely bruised ribs. Pittsburgh won that game, but missed the AFC title encounter with Oakland. The Steelers went down 24-7 and

Harris had an eye for the opening and would sometimes step out of bounds rather than take an unnecessary hit.

rushed for a total of just 72 yards.

Pittsburgh would ask for increasingly more mileage out of Harris. His next two seasons saw him carry the ball a total of 610 times — a mark of their reliance on his power and durability.

A third Super Bowl win in 1979 saw Harris score on a 22-yard run and he actually got two more TDs in the fourth world title victory the following season.

The quietly-spoken Harris (his press interviews were given at a level less than a whisper) let the brasher personalities on the super Steelers team look after the PR end of the job. He let his rushing talk for him.

But as the title team began to break up, Harris's role began to change. He was asked to be a target of more passes (he finished his Steeler career as their fourth-best in history) and his rushing figures suffered.

However, when given the ball often enough, he could still pull out the 1,000-yard years, as he did in his final season at Pittsburgh in 1983. A contract dispute after that year meant a sad end to his career at Pittsburgh. He tried to perform for one season at Seattle, but without success.

It should have been his glory year. The one in which he became the NFL's all-time leading rusher, but instead he was beaten to it by Chicago's Walter Payton and never even got past the great Jim Brown's total.

Such an unhappy ending shouldn't hide the fact that Harris's muscular style, slippery speed and eye for daylight was the basis of one team's greatest moments. His career ran parallel with Pittsburgh's golden years. True, he played behind an outstanding offensive line, but when he wasn't there, the Steelers always looked a poorer team. And when Pittsburgh needed that something extra on a third and short, there was never any question that Franco Harris had that little bit necessary to get the job done.

★★★ Franco Harris ★★★

Runningback. 6ft 2in, 225 lb. Born in Fort Dix, New Jersey, 7 March 1950. Attended Penn State University. 1972-83 Pittsburgh Steelers, 1984 Seattle Seahawks.

Through most of his thirteen years of training and playing, Harris kept himself at the top of the rushing lists.

Rushing statistics

Year	Attempts	Yards	Average	Touchdowns
+ 1972	188	1,055	5.6	10
+ 1973	188	698	3.7	3
+ 1974	208	1,006	4.8	5
+ 1975	262	1,246	4.8	10
+ 1976	289	1,128	3.9	14
+ 1977	300	1,162	3.9	11
+ 1978	310	1,082	3.5	8
+ 1979	267	1,186	4.4	11
+ 1980	208	789	3.8	4
+ 1981	242	987	4.1	8
+ 1982	140	604	4.3	2
+ 1983	279	1,007	3.6	5
● 1984	68	170	2.5	0
Total	**2,949**	**12,020**	**40**	**91**

+ with Pittsburgh Steelers
● with Seattle Seahawks

Receiving: 307 catches, 2,287 yards, 7.5 yard average, 9 touchdowns

Elroy Hirsch
Crazylegs

his crazy-legs style helped him to greatness

The long bomb is a passing option that the fans love. The speedster receiver jets downfield and takes an over-his-shoulder pass in mid-stride. If such a pass goes for a touchdown, then it registers a 'Wow' on the 'Amazing Scale'.

If it happens nine times in one season, then there isn't any scale to measure such an achievement. Especially since it happened in the 1950s when QBs were not as throw-happy as they are in the 1980s. Elroy Hirsch achieved ten long bomb TDs in 1951, from 34, 44, 47, 53, 70, 72, 76, 79, 81 and 91 yards — an average of over 64 yards per catch.

It sounds easy, put down in print, but Hirsch's story was one of continual struggle, particularly in the early days.

As a skinny high school kid, Elroy didn't even make the team.

Hirsch joined the Los Angeles Ram in 1949 and made an immediate impact.

As a halfback, Hirsch didn't lack courage or technique.

Eventually, after gaining some weight and improving his sidestep ability by rushing full-sprint through a local wood during practice sessions, he was good enough to play for the University of Wisconsin. He enjoyed considerable success, rushing out of the backfield and passing as well. But, in 1943, the Second World War moved him to the University of Michigan as a Marine. There he proved his all-round talents by playing in football, basketball, baseball and athletics teams.

But it was his tie-up with the Marines that indirectly could have cut short a glittering gridiron career. Hirsch had been drafted by the NFL Cleveland Rams as a 'future' in 1945, but when he came out of the services one year later, Elroy turned them down. Instead, he chose to sign up for the new All America Football Conference team, the Chicago Hornets, whom were coached by a man named Dick Hanley for whom Hirsch had played in the Marines' team. It was a decision he'd always regret.

The Hornets were A1 awful and Elroy called his time with them 'three frightful years'. During that time he was asked to be a one-man team — rushing from halfback, catching passes, returning all kicks and playing defense, too. The jobs took their toll. Torn back muscles and damaged knee ligaments restricted his performances until a fractured skull in 1948 almost ended them forever.

The blow had come behind his right ear and for months it looked as if he'd never play again since his co-ordination was affected. But his hope was that he could join the Rams (by now playing in Los Angeles) when his AAFC contract expired. Elroy kept up the rehabilitative work and got his wish in 1949. However, his run of injuries didn't help when it came to unseating the crop of capable Ram runningbacks already at the club.

His coach, the famed Clark Shaughnessy, held Hirsch back and more often used him as a second or a decoy on passing downs. It wasn't until a new coach (Joe Stydahar) came to the Rams in 1950 that Elroy was given a chance at end, the principal pass-catching position of that period.

Yet, things still didn't work out right as Hirsch tried to settle into a new position. Time and again inexperience meant he ended up empty-handed on the floor rather than downfield with the ball in his grasp. But the never-give-in attitude that had allowed Hirsch to come back from injury served him well once more. By the end of the '50 season, Elroy had grabbed seven TDs out of 42 catches for 687 yards. The next season would put all bad memories behind him forever.

That 1951 season was a championship year for the Rams and a banner year for Hirsch — he was their undoubted star. He reeled off

A finger-tip catch and Hirsch was on his way to another touchdown.

those long-bomb touchdowns as if it was child's play. His nickname of 'Crazylegs' (which had actually been given to him while at college in Wisconsin) was now in every sports page headline.

Those wildly-girating legs made his running style unique. His speciality was the over-the-shoulder catch at top speed — no one did it better.

He and fellow receiver Tom Fears were an unstoppable combination in 1951 and, although Fears took the honours in the championship game win over Cleveland by scoring the winning TD, Hirsch was the man of the season. Elroy accounted for seventeen out of the rams 51 touchdowns that year — one third of their total. He clocked up 66 receptions during the year for 1,495 yards at an astonishing average of 22.7 yards per catch. The touchdown and total yardage marks still stand as Rams records.

Hirsch was the first player to emulate the man who was his own boyhood hero, Don Hutson, the true inventor of football pass receiving. Elroy's seventeen TD catches in '51 equalled Hutson's own record (unbeaten until 1984) and confirmed the rise of the importance of the pass.

The Rams had some fine players in those days which made Hirsch's job a little easier, but there was no doubting his greatness.

Those 'Crazylegs' carried him on until 1957 when age finally got the better of him after twelve pro years. Hirsch had to fight long and hard for those years and for the glory that they brought. For the 1951 season alone, it was all worth it.

★★★ **Elroy (Crazylegs) Hirsch** ★★★

Halfback-end. 6ft 2in, 190 lb. Born in Wausau, Wisconsin, 17 June 1923. Attended University of Wisconsin, Michigan. 1946-48 Chicago Rockets (AAFC), 1949-57 Los Angeles Rams.

Receiving statistics

Year	Receptions	Yards	Average	Touchdowns
+ 1946	27	347	12.9	3
+ 1947	10	282	28.2	3
+ 1948	7	101	14.4	1
● 1949	22	326	14.8	4
● 1950	42	687	16.4	7
● 1951	66	1495	22.7	17
● 1952	25	590	23.6	4
● 1953	61	941	15.4	4
● 1954	35	720	20.6	3
● 1955	25	460	18.4	2
● 1956	35	603	17.2	6
● 1957	32	477	14.9	6
Total	**387**	**7029**	**18.2**	**60**

+ with Chicago Rockets
● with Los Angeles Rams

Rushing: 74 attempts, 317 yards, 4.3 average, 2 touchdowns

Sam Huff
The Hard Man

a linebacker who knew how to hit hardest

In the 1950s Sam Huff was one half of the greatest confrontation the NFL had ever seen. Huff was granite-hard with a passion for dynamite hitting of his opponents. When he played opposite Cleveland's Jim Brown sparks would fly and a nation would look on in awe. For Brown was pro football's mightiest runningback and Huff was its most tenacious linebacker.

This regular clash of the titans helped mould the Huff philosophy: 'You play as hard and as tough as you can but you play clean. We hit each other hard, sure. But this is a man's game and any guy who doesn't want to hit hard doesn't belong in it.'

Huff was the NFL's most competitive middle linebacker ever. He had dedication, a love for the sport and a rare perception on the field.

In his heyday, Huff's face appeared on the cover of *Time* magazine.

But Sam Huff had to overcome a series of career crises before he made it big. Huff was only spotted by a college scout by mistake (the scout was eyeing another player) and the same thing happened to take him to the Giants as a third round draft pick from West Virginia. Once in New York, however, Sam had another problem — no one knew which was his best position. Huff even left training camp once and considered quitting only to be coaxed back by Giants defensive coach at the time Vince Lombardi.

An injury to the first string middle linebacker gave Huff the chance he needed in the opening game of the 1956 season. He impressed so much in that most important of positions that he made it his own.

Sam began to shine brightly under the New York spotlight. The city is always hungry for heroes and Huff appeared on the cover of Time magazine, he was the subject of a TV special entitled 'The Violent World of Sam Huff' and would later be one of four NFL players chosen to tour Vietnam on a special troop visit.

In the fifties he led the fierce Giants defense and his team reached six NFL finals in eight years (unfortunately they only won once). But in 1963, after another championship game defeat, rumours about too many Giants getting too old began to circulate. Before the next season started, Huff had been traded to Washington.

The move left Sam angry and disheartened — he'd been loved by Giants fans and he loved the club. However, the Redskins offered him a good contract and he again put off thoughts of retiring. Huff brought extra muscle to the Washington defense but after $3\frac{1}{2}$ seasons he suffered a severe ankle injury. It caused him to miss the last four games of the season — the first he'd missed since he became a pro.

The injury was so bad that Huff quit — but only for a year. He came back to the Redskins as player-coach in 1969 when Vince Lombardi joined the club. Loyalty to the great coach who had saved his career at New York was a major reason for the change of mind. So when Lombardi tragically died in 1970, Huff's playing and coaching career also ended.

Sam had been one of the great defensive players of the era — nothing short of a national idol. But it could have been so different. He grew up in a coal mining area of West Virginia and only missed becoming a miner by a whisker. 'A coach came to our high school game to see another guy named Rudy. The coach picked me instead

When Huff wasn't crashing into runningbacks he was intercepting passes. His career total was thirty.

and it was Rudy who ended up down the mine,' recalls Sam.

Huff took that never-give-up attitude into the pros where he changed the role of all middle linebackers. Rather than just plug the nearest hole in the line, Sam shot hither and thither after the man with the ball. That was something no other linebacker could do consistently. He had the athletic ability to hold the most powerful fullbacks, catch the swiftest halfbacks and cover most short-range passes.

His mentor, Vince Lombardi, paid him this compliment: 'It's uncanny the way Huff follows the ball. He ignores all the things you do to get him away from the play and he comes after the ball wherever it's thrown or wherever the run goes. He seems to be all over the field at once.'

★★★ Sam Huff ★★★

Linebacker. 6ft 1in, 230 lb. Born in Morgantown, West Virginia, 4 October 1934. Attended West Virginia University. 1956-63 New York Giants, 1964-67, 1969 Washington Redskins.

Interception record: 1956-63 at NY Giants, 18 interceptions, 208 yards, 11.5 yard average, 1 touchdown. 1964-69 at Washington, 12 interceptions, 173 yards, 14.4 yard average, 1 touchdown. Career, 30 interceptions, 381 yards, 12.7 yard average, 2 touchdowns.

Don Hutson
The Alabama Antelope
one of the gridiron game's true innovators

There are only a handful of true innovators in any sport. In the history of American football, Don Hutson is one of them. He was simply way ahead of his time. Hutson took hold of part of the game and turned it into an art form. He could glide past defenders with feints and shimmies, leap with almost balletic grace and cradle the ball in his so-safe hands. He was the first true pass receiver.

Born in Pine Bluff, Arkansas, he took his slim 6 ft 1 in frame to the University of Alabama, where he made a reputation for turning an ordinary pass into an extraordinary gain. By 1935 Don turned to the pro league and had been signed by both the Green Bay Packers and Brooklyn Dodgers. The NFL had to decide which team would get him. Both contracts arrived at their office on the same day. The Packers' had been postmarked seventeen minutes earlier — that was the decider.

In those days the game was played on the ground and passes were scorned by purists. Hutson's inventiveness in running a pattern rather than just in a straight line changed that concept. Some people took a lot of convincing. New Brooklyn coach Jock Sutherland was one such man. He did not believe in double or triple marking pass receivers but when Hutson caught two TD passes against the Dodgers in a super display, Sutherland's mind was changed.

Hutson had even caught his first ever NFL pass and run it in for a TD. He would compile career statistics which would stand almost untouchable for decades and are still worthy even today. In his second season (1936), Hutson won the first of his three NFL titles. He caught the opening TD pass (a 50-yarder) as the Pack beat the Boston Redskins. Green Bay won again three years later and Hutson complete a hat-trick in his penultimate year. During those games and in most of the matches he played in, Hutson would be double or even triple-teamed — something unheard of for a receiver in those days.

Hutson's receiving statistics would even stand up against some of today's top pass catchers.

Even more incredible is the fact that Hutson was in the game at a time when every player had to be a sixty-minute man. There was no separate offense, defense and special teams, the pre-war players had to do it all. On defense Don was a fine safety who could pick off interceptions to opponents just as effortlessly as he picked off any passes to himself. In his later years he even developed into a reliable placekicker, scoring 200 points. During one game he caught four TD passes and kicked five extra points for a total of 29 points — in just one quarter of play.

Perhaps his one regret is that he missed the Packers' two golden periods of the early thirties and mid-sixties. In his eleven-year career Green Bay had eleven winning seasons but only three NFL titles (in 1936, '39 and '44). Nevertheless his individual mark was indelibly made.

On any given day, Don Hutson could walk onto a football field with black boot polish daubed on his cheekbones to cut out the glare of the afternoon sun (something else he invented) and give football fans of his age a glimpse of what was to come. The days of multi-receiver offenses was well in the distant future. Don Hutson — the man nicknamed the Alabama Antelope — was already there.

★★★   Don Hutson   ★★★

End. 6ft 1in, 180 lb. Born in Pine Bluff, Arkansas, 31 January 1913. Attended University of Alabama. 1935-45 Green Bay Packers.

Receiving statistics

Year	Games	Receipts	Yards	Average	Touchdowns
1935	10	18	420	23.3	6
1936	12	34	536	15.8	9
1937	11	41	552	13.5	7
1938	10	32	548	17.1	9
1939	11	34	846	24.9	6
1940	11	45	664	14.8	7
1941	11	58	738	12.7	10
1942	11	74	1211	16.4	17
1943	10	47	776	16.5	11
1944	10	58	866	14.9	9
1945	10	47	834	17.7	9
Total	**117**	**488**	**7,991**	**16.4**	**100**

Rushing: 74 attempts, 317 yards, 4.3 average and 2 touchdowns.

David 'Deacon' Jones
The Deacon
an unknown who got himself noticed

If you want to get noticed on the gridiron, you have to be exciting. That was the philosophy of David 'Deacon' Jones and he lived it to the full. You couldn't help but notice the man, he was probably the greatest defensive end football's ever had. That's because he took the position of DE and made it almost like a second offense.

Jones didn't wait for the runningbacks to come to his side of the field — he chased after *them*. And quarterbacks began to get the jitters with him on the field. He coined the term 'sack' for a tackle on the QB and took pleasure in the act for fourteen seasons.

He was one part of the LA Rams' 'Fearsome Foursome' defensive line of the sixties. Along with Merlin Olsen, Jones made the left side of that line a no-go area and, as blindside pass rushers to most QBs, they created unheard-of problems for opponents who tried to counter by double or even triple-teaming Jones. Usually it was in vain.

Jones disregarded the fact that defensive end was an unglamourous position right at the beginning of his career. He started by calling himself 'Deacon'. 'No one would remember a player named David Jones,' he said. 'I picked out "Deacon" because it would be remembered in the violent pro football world.

That happened in Jones' first year at the Rams where he was a fourteenth round draft pick. Two scouts had spotted him at a tiny Mississippi college when they were originally looking at a runningback.

The Rams late-round gamble paid off handsomely. Jones surprised everybody except himself by making the squad and went on to be named the team's rookie of the year. Deacon had introduced himself to the NFL with a mighty clatter.

He thought up the term 'sack' in college ('You know, you sack a city — you devastate it'). Defensive players now had a clear term to prove their effectiveness — a sack meant excitement and began to get them noticed more and more. Jones used his own publicity trick

Jones was the meanest man in the Ram 'Fearsome Foursome'.

to the full. In 1967 (around the peak of his career), Deacon registered more sacks of his own (26) than entire teams of opponents did on the Rams QB (25).

He wasn't the type of guy to let this go unnoticed either. The press lapped up his brash statements and Jones continually hit the headlines — sometimes for his off the field activities as well.

The man they named the 'Secretary of Defense' was a technician as well as a publicist. He developed the 'slap' — an open-handed

Closing in on Green Bay's Bart Starr is Jones (75) and his fellow Rams.

blow to the head of an opposing lineman. This move often gave Jones the split second extra he needed. Eventually the head slap was outlawed.

Another innovation was the loop or stunt. Jones and Olsen would cause mass confusion just before the snap by changing places on the line of scrimmage — Olsen would loop to the outside and Jones come inside. In 1970, such moves brought the Rams 53 sacks.

It was this emphasis on mobility which was new to defensive line play. Deacon was as big as necessary (6ft 4in and nearly 18 stone), but that bulk was all agility and he was able to move as quickly as a runningback. He delighted in proving his speed and, one time, went stride-for-stride with one of the fastest players of his time, Bobby Mitchell. Jones raced alongside Mitchell after he caught a pass. The two shot down the sideline side-by-side for about ten yards before Deacon pushed his man out of bounds. 'I just wanted to see if I was as fast as he was,' the Deacon said.

Unfortunately for Jones, the Rams never reached the heights of

Super Bowls and the like despite a defense that set an NFL record low for yardage conceded in 1968. His coaching mentor at LA had been George Allen and when the coach left, Jones decided to go as well. Two seasons with San Diego were tough because the Chargers had a pitiful team at that time and Deacon was fighting a losing battle.

For his final season in 1974, Jones linked up again with Allen at Washington. The Redskins were consistent play-off placers and Deacon hoped for ultimate glory in his last year.

True to form, the Skins made the play-offs, but who should they lose to in the first post-season hurdle? Of course, it was the LA Rams.

After that, Jones called it a day. He had played in eight Pro Bowls and been runner-up for the league's MVP award on one occasion.

Fourteen rugged seasons at the very top of his profession had got David 'Deacon' Jones noticed alright. Certainly, no one who ever played against him can forget.

★★★   David (Deacon) Jones   ★★★

Defensive end. 6ft 5in, 250 lb. Born in Eatonville, Florida, 9 December 1938. Attended South Carolina State and Mississippi Vocational Colleges. 1961-71 Los Angeles Rams, 1972-73 San Diego Chargers, 1974 Washington Redskins.

Jack Lambert
Mad Jack
a chip off the old Steeler block

Pittsburgh is a tough, tough city of steel, noise and grime. Its football team has to reflect its blue-collar values. So do its football players and Jack Lambert was the epitome of those values.

His position at middle linebacker required the mentality of a contract killer — he would go for his man with an alarming fury that ended in the crash of helmet on bone. Lambert was a superb role model for those steelworking fans as he got rid of their frustrations by proxy on the gridiron. He wasn't adverse to helping out on the frustration front in some smokey Pittsburgh bar-room either, when the situation called for a brawl. Lambert was truly just one of the boys.

His linebacking position meant he had to be in on everything — and he was. Lambert was a dominant player on defense. There was

★

A youthful-looking Lambert soon became an integral part of the Steel Curtain.

★

Above This interception in Super Bowl XIV assured the Steelers of their fourth title.
Left As a middle linebacker, Lambert was everywhere — either tackling runners or deflecting passes.

no linebacking duty at which he didn't excel.

At 6ft 4in and a modest 220 lb, he could cover the passing zones like an octopus and he could fill up the running lanes like a concrete wall.

Lambert played in one of the most consistent winning teams of all-time. Both offense and defense were chock-a-block with famous names. He arrived at the club just in time to be part of it all.

He was the Steelers second round draft choice in '74 (receiver Lynn Swann was their first) and soon proved himself to be a worthy member of the Steel Curtain defense which was adding to its fearsome reputation with every game. Lambert didn't get a starting job automatically, but by the time Pittsburgh got to their first Super Bowl, he was irreplaceable. That Super Bowl (like all the others involving Pittsburgh in the seventies) ended in a Steelers victory. Lambert was named defensive rookie of the year and in his second season he became the leader of the Steeler defense from his pivotal position.

In his second season, he won his second Super Bowl ring. Colleagues pointed to Lambert as the man who held the defense together in an uncompromising style. He could intimidate a whole team on his own.

The '76 season ended without a Super Bowl, but Lambert's defense did more-than-normal duty by keeping the injury-hit Steelers in with a chance. Their record on the run-in to that year's play-offs speaks for itself — 22 quarters without conceding a touchdown, five of the last eight opponents were shut-out and only one team in the last nine games scored a TD against them. In the AFC title game, Jack recovered three fumbles for an NFL record, but it wasn't enough and the Steelers lost to Oakland.

Lambert's performances were noted and in 1977 he was made defensive captain. A year later a third Super Bowl ring was added to his collection. However, it was 1979 which became his banner year.

He led the NFL in interceptions with six and was named the league's defensive player of the year for the second time.

Yet, it was his effect in the fourth Pittsburgh Super Bowl appearance that will be most clearly remembered. In one play, he chased LA Rams running back Wendell Tyler across the field for a nine-yard loss and then pulled off a crucial interception.

Pittsburgh were under the kosh at the time. The Rams had the momentum of the game late in the fourth quarter. Another pass was on its way to a Rams receiver when Lambert got in front of the target and clasped the ball to his chest. He then ran sixteen yards to get his team out of the danger zone and virtually seal their victory. He was the kind of defensive player who could often turn the whole team around on one play, such was his intensity.

Over the next couple of seasons, his fellow Steel Curtain defenders began to retire with frequency (he had been the youngest member when he joined their ranks in '74) and Pittsburgh turned from a 4-3 defense to a 3-4. Lambert made the transition with ease and continued to lead his team in tackles — he did so in everyone of his first ten seasons.

Injuries, however, were beginning to trouble him. He rarely missed a game at first, but the position of linebacker requires total physical perfection and after eleven seasons he was forced to retire.

His legacy was one of distinction. He played in nine Pro Bowls and won such admiration from his fellow professionals that they placed him among the ranks of the greats in his position.

Lambert looked like a tough linebacker with his droopy moustache (which he grew later in his career) and battle-scarred features. His wild-stare eyes and missing front teeth gave him a look of madness needed for his role in pro football. He was also the type of guy you'd chose to walk into a fight with. A never-let-you-down hero who inspired by incredible deeds. He could lift others around him to ever higher peaks of performance. Considering the heights that the Steeler defense achieved during his reign of terror, Lambert's effect on football may never be matched.

★★★   **Jack Lambert**   ★★★

Linebacker. 6ft 4in, 220 lb. Born in Mantua, Ohio, 8 July 1952. Attended Kent State. 1974-84 Pittsburgh Steelers.

Dick Lane
Night Train

perfected the art of the cornerback

'Night Train' Lane was a player who put fear into the eyes of receivers. He would stalk his prey with the cunning of a fox. His movements were quick and agile. His hitting almost seemed to cut men in half. For fourteen years, Lane prowled the passing zones perfecting a new art — that of cornerbacking. The game itself was in a period of transition and Lane had to develop the style of covering receivers from scratch.

During his career, quarterbacks were beginning to increase their number of passes significantly. This merely increased Lane's effectiveness. It culminated in Night Train being named as the NFL's all-time best cornerback in 1969 by the Pro Hall of Fame.

Lane learned his football at a small Nebraska college and during four years in the army. The LA Rams signed him as a free agent in 1952 and the nervous rookie (a little bit older than most first-year men at 24) would often hunt out veteran receiver Tom Fears for advice.

Fear's favourite record at the time was a fifties standard called *Night Train*. The song was always playing in his room when Dick Lane arrived seeking words of wisdom. 'Here comes Night Train,' they used to say and the nickname stuck. All that advice from Fears must have done some good because Night Train's first season as a pro was covered in glory.

He grabbed fourteen interceptions — a pro record which has never yet been beaten. It is more remarkable when you realize that the ball wasn't passed nearly as often as it is today (a modern-day cornerback would be delirious with just ten interceptions).

But the fame didn't stop there. Lane, a 200 lb, 6ft 2in, wiry sort of guy, decided that ferocity would become the key. He invented something called the necktie tackle. It was Lane's way of stopping hulking great runningbacks as well as the nimble-footed receivers.

Instead of aiming for the knees, Night Train thundered into his man high — and hard. On occasion, such a tackle would send the

Night Train Lane prowled the pass zones like a fox for fourteen years.

unfortunate player, the ball and probably the helmet all flying off in different directions.

After two years at LA, Lane took his talents on to the Chicago Cardinals (later to move themselves to St Louis). His six seasons there were less happy apart from 1954 when he picked off ten passes. Lane's own form dived as he accused the team of not being dedicated to winning.

Night Train was traded to Detroit in 1960, and, at the age of 32, some Lions fans thought he was over the hill. Instead, Lane was better than ever. He revelled in the Lions man-to-man coverage and perfected his death-or-glory style. Many plays seemed like a gamble

Lane's greatest years were with the Detroit Lions in the sixties.

— either Night Train intercepted and ran for a touchdown or the receiver made the big play and got the score. Gripping stuff.

The role of the cornerback was now an accepted one in football as offenses looked to the pass. But if the role of the cornerback was accepted then Lane's play wasn't — it was always called unorthodox.

There was really no other player like him. Night Train made up the rules for his position as he went along. Only age put a stop to his dominance — he retired aged 37.

Unfortunately, the Lions form during the Lane era produced neither divisional titles nor NFL championships. What it did produce was some memorable games, some fascinating confrontations and one of the most innovative players in football history.

★★★ Dick (Night Train) Lane ★★★

Defensive Back. 6ft 2in, 210 lb. Born in Austin, Texas, 16 April 1928. Attended Scottsbluff Junior College. 1952-53 Los Angeles Rams, 1954-59 Chicago Cardinals, 1960-65 Detroit Lions.

Interception statistics

Year	Interceptions	Yards	Average	Touchdowns
+ 1952	14	298	21.3	2
+ 1953	3	9	3.0	0
* 1954	10	181	18.1	0
* 1955	6	69	11.5	0
* 1956	7	206	29.4	1
* 1957	2	47	23.5	0
* 1958	2	0	0.0	0
* 1959	3	125	41.7	1
● 1960	5	102	20.4	1
● 1961	6	73	12.2	0
● 1962	4	16	4.0	0
● 1963	5	70	14.0	0
● 1964	1	11	11.0	0
● 1965	0	0	0.0	0
Total	**68**	**1,207**	**17.8**	**5**

+ with Los Angeles Rams
* with Chicago Cardinals
● with Detroit Lions

Bob Lilly
Mr Cowboy
a classic Dallas Cowboy

When a new team is born in the NFL, there are many factors which need to gell if it's to become successful. Sound administrating, consistent coaching and, not least, inspired playing.

The Dallas Cowboys were born in 1960 with an unshakable Texan desire to rise to the cream of their profession. The owners had confidence in their ability, they appointed a resilient young coach in Tom Landry, but what of the third less controllable element? Fortunately for the Dallas franchise within a year, they chose a gem as their first-ever player from the college draft. Bob Lilly had been an All-American defensive lineman at Texas Christian.

He was a local boy who was overjoyed to be able to star for his local team. It proved to be a match made in heaven. Lilly would make the position of defensive tackle seem as if it was made for him and only him. He would lead the Dallas franchise to magnificent peaks and ensure that the team remained at the top-most level throughout his career and beyond.

His selection was often referred to by Coach Landry as the best move he ever made in those formative Cowboy days.

Dallas began life as just another expansion team. Their playing squad in their opening season of 1960 was made up of veterans from other NFL teams. It wasn't until 1961 that they could participate in the college draft.

The first season had been a pitiful 0-11-1 experience — one tie in twelve games. The bunch of give-away veterans needed new blood. They needed a leader. In Bob Lilly they got one.

For two seasons, however, this wasn't quite so apparent. Lilly was playing defensive end and wasn't having too much impact on the opposing offenses. He had to adjust to Coach Landry's complex flex defense, it was true, but there was more to it than that. Perhaps a change of position was called for?

Lilly was put in at defensive tackle and the improvement was immediate. That season finished with the new DT in the Pro Bowl

Lilly provided the Cowboys with much-needed leadership on the gridiron.

for the first time. He would play in the post-season extravaganza on 10 more occasions. It was his great strength combined with ultra-quick reactions that made him such a better interior defensive lineman. Against slightly lighter men (rather than hulking offensive tackles), Lilly could often burst into the backfield.

The man and his team were on the rise. By 1966 the Cowboys were divisional champions and on a seemingly never-ending winning streak. Lilly was a key figure in their first Super Bowl appearance after the 1970 regular season. When Dallas lost to a last second field goal, there was little Lilly could do.

However, a year later, in Super Bowl VI, there was more he could do . . . and did. The Cowboys weren't going to be denied again and they seemed much more aggressive and ready for a scrap. Bob Lilly demonstrated that in one particular play. He shot through the Miami offensive line and set his eyes on QB Bob Griese. After a zigzag chase, Lilly got his man a full 29 yards behind the line of scrimmage.

Such a loss set the tone for the game and Lilly's defense conceded just one field goal all day. The man they called 'Mr Cowboy' had a Super Bowl ring.

In his final three seasons, Lilly showed few signs of easing down. He was the definitive Cowboy in that respect.

A clean-cut, God-fearing man, Lilly worked extra-hard to master his craft. After a leg injury in 1973, he put himself through an off-season fitness programme that many younger men would never undertake. It prepared him for a final season of football that was just as important to him as his first. Lilly wanted the best from himself so he could do his best for the team. That's a true Cowboy concept. 'I'd much rather miss the All-Pro team and have the Cowboys win,' he once said.

In the season following his retirement (1975), the Cowboys retired his no 74 jersey and Lilly became the club's first Pro Hall of Famer four years later.

Tributes had been bestowed on him throughout a fourteen-year assault on opposing defenses. They remarked always on both his quickness of action and thought. Those were his most impressive attributes. His durability was also a testimony to his dedication. Lilly never missed a regular season game in his career. It was missing the NFC title game in 1973 (the only one he ever did miss) with a leg injury that spurred on that pre-74 massive training programme.

How much influence can a defensive tackle command on a gridiron? This one commanded a whole lot. Teams would actually run plays straight at him, thereby neutralizing his pursuit speed and agility. That's one hell of a back-handed compliment.

Lilly was the foundation of the Dallas Doomsday Defense and proved to be the very symbol of the club. His coach, Tom Landry, paid him this ultimate tribute: 'There won't be another Bob Lilly in my time. A player like him comes along once in a coach's lifetime. You're observing a man who will become a legend.'

★★★ Bob Lilly ★★★

Defensive tackle. 6ft 5in, 260 lb. Born in Olney, Texas, 24 July, 1939. Attended Texas Christian University. 1961-74 Dallas Cowboys.

Vince Lombardi
The Greatest

a coach who never had a losing season

There are good coaches, there are great coaches and then there's Vince Lombardi. The man who won pro football's first two Super Bowl crowns was the embodiment of the desire to win and its most effective executioner.

His sayings are endless and legendary. Perhaps the one that best summed up his devotion to the game was: 'Winning isn't everything — it's the *only* thing'.

His dedication to the job was immense. His long-time quarterback Bart Starr once commented: 'We all knew that he bled inside for us, he just loved us'.

His effect on the game itself is unquestionable. In just nine seasons at Green Bay, Lombardi was five times NFL champion and twice Super Bowl winner. Only a cruel early death from cancer at the age of 57 prevented further triumphs. But his name will never be forgotten, he was honoured after his death when the Super Bowl trophy was named after him.

The Lombardi philosophy was based on hard work and stressed the perfect execution of relatively simple plays. He worked his players like demons (some players said it was more like dogs), but only because of his own tremendous dedication. He won his coaching spurs as an assistant with the New York Giants and was 45-years-old before he took charge at Green Bay as head coach and general manager. 'I'm in complete command here,' he said. And never was there any doubt that he was.

Lombardi took over a miserable team with a 1-10 record, but he made one thing clear from the start. 'I've never been on a dog team,' he told his players, 'and I have no intention of starting now.' The Packers went back to basics and extra-long practice sessions startled players and fans. Yet, it soon became apparent that the system worked.

In his first season in charge (1959), Lombardi guided the team to a 7-5 record, their best for fifteen years. The Packers era began in

Main picture Packer players carry their coach from the field after Super Bowl II — Lombardi's last with Green Bay.

Right This was the sight that Packer players so often saw on their sideline — a bellowing Lombardi in coat and hat.

Far right Lombardi had only ten seasons as a head coach before he died of cancer in 1970.

earnest the following season when they surprisingly won the Western Division only to come up short in the NFL championship game. Green Bay would never come up short again when a title was on the line.

Ironically, Lombardi's Packers got the chance to show their mettle the next season (1961) against the New York Giants who had given them their saviour. The Pack won by a devastating 37-0 and then repeated the dose (this time 16-7) in 1962 for a second championship in a row.

In 1963, Lombardi's plans for a hat-trick of titles were hit by a ban on his all-purpose halfback Paul Hornung and they lost out for a title spot by half a game.

It wasn't until the '65 season that things got back to 'normal' and Green Bay were champions again. Then came the first two Super Bowls and the Packers won them both with ease. Lombardi had built a wonderful team. He could be seen on the sidelines yelling and shouting, encouraging the players whom he called 'artists, not truck drivers'.

He was regarded as an innovator, but his basic plays — the strong side sweep and the weak side slant — were bread and butter running plays. It was his motivation that counted for more. 'Win a team's heart and they'll follow you anywhere, do the impossible for you,' said this most-quoted of coaches.

But, after winning everything in sight at Green Bay, Lombardi himself needed a new job for his personal motivation.

He left the Packers a year after winning Super Bowl II to become part-owner, vice-president, general manager and head coach at Washington. The Redskins' won-loss record at the time was as sad as Green Bay's had been back in 1958. That was just how Lombardi liked it.

He soon installed a classic running game as Washington went back to the basics, Lombardi-style. Nothing fancy, just winning football. Redskin fans hadn't seen a winning season since 1955, Lombardi gave it to them in his first year at the helm.

But health began to give up on the great man. He died two weeks before the start of the 1970 season and the football world was stunned by the death of a man who had put such life into the teams he coached.

Overall, his teams won 105 matches out of 146 — which adds up to almost three out of every four. His record in play-off games was even more stunning — nine wins out of ten. Few experts doubted that Lombardi was the greatest pro coach of all-time. He never had a losing season.

His players felt the lashing of his tongue and they sweated through his taskmaster style of training. But they adored him. Lombardi was the nearest thing pro football has ever had to a certain winner. His reign as the master was quite short, but during it, he won every honour in the game and the heart of every person that knew him.

★★★   Vince Lombardi   ★★★

Coach. Born in Brooklyn, New York, June 11, 1913. Died 3 September 1970. Attended Fordham University. Inducted in 1971. 1959-67 Green Bay Packers, 1969 Washington Redskins.

Team statistics

Year	Team	Record	Year	Team	Record
1959	Green Bay	7-5-0	1965*	Green Bay	10-3-1
1960	Green Bay	8-4-0	1966*	Green Bay	12-2-0
1961*	Green Bay	11-3-0	1967*	Green Bay	9-4-1
1962*	Green Bay	13-1-0	1968	Retired	
1963	Green Bay	11-2-1	1969	Washington	7-5-2
1964	Green Bay	8-5-1	Total		**96-34-6**

Note: regular season only

* Championship seasons

Sid Luckman
The Pass Master
many say there's never been a better quarterback

In the eighties the pass kings are Montana and Marino. In the forties it was Luckman and Baugh. Sid Luckman and Sammy Baugh were the first real masters of the football airways. They were the first men to put the game on the way to the current pass-crazy era.

Slingin' Sammy threw almost all day and, thereby, set many of the early passing records in categories such as attempts, completions and yardage. But to rate him no 1 of his time is to look only at statistics. Luckman left the stats for others and, instead, came out on top in a different category — winning NFL titles.

In twelve seasons Sid took the Bears to four championships — double the number that Baugh won in sixteen years. It was those kinds of facts which got Luckman his nickname of 'Mister Quarterback'.

Yet Luckman was just a tailback at Columbia University. It was Bears legendary coach George Halas who turned Sid into one of the smartest signal callers and slickest ball handlers the NFL had ever seen. Halas had co-invented the T-formation for his beloved Chicago with its three runningbacks standing in a line parallel to the scrimmage and a split end out wide for the pass.

By 1939 the system was seen as archaic. Halas didn't agree and began making the T-formation increasingly intricate. First he brought in the man-in-motion and then he got Luckman. Just a year after these two elements were joined, Chicago won their first NFL title for seven years — and what a game it was.

The Bears devastated Sammy Baugh and his Redskins 73-0. The once-rejected T-formation shot back to prominence and Sid Luckman wasn't far behind. That day changed Luckman's life and he remembered it as something special. 'There was a feeling of tension in the air as though something tremendous was about to happen.'

A year later Luckman and the Bears did it again, this time a 37-9 win over the NY Giants in the title game.

Luckman's 14,683 passing yards came when throwing the football was still something of a novelty.

Runners-up in 1942, Sid and his men were back to the top a year later and it was a truly great year for Luckman himself. In a match against the Giants Sid threw seven touchdown passes and also became the first pro player to throw for more than 400 yards in a game. His final total that day was 433. In beating the Redskins again in the championship game of 1943, Luckman hurled five TD passes and he was then voted the league's MVP.

There would be one more title-winning performance by Sid in 1946 when he wrapped up the game with his first and only TD run of that season. Coach Halas had called a trap play on the Giants 19-yard line. The call so surprised Luckman that he asked for a time-out. He went over to check the call and Halas confirmed his decision. Dutifully, Sid faked his hand-off, ran right and off into the end zone.

After this seaon of triumph, Luckman would have only one more year at the top. That was the following season when he threw for a personal best of 31 TDs which was also the highest in the NFL. Younger men (like Hall-of-Famer-to-be Bobby Layne) were now

Sid would launch his passes and also propel the Bears towards titles.

coming through to challenge Luckman's position and he saw less and less action in his final three seasons.

During his career Sid also did his share of punting (he had a best season-long average of 41 yards in 1941) and playing defense (he intercepted fourteen passes and ran back one for a TD) but he retired after the 1950 season to serve as quarterback coach.

Looking back, his playing career was wrapped up with Halas and the T-formation but he undoubtedly left his individual mark on the sport. Luckman's leadership qualities on the field were unrivalled at the time. The pundits thought he won as many games with his head as he did with his arm.

He didn't throw as many passes as some fellas but he had a better touchdown-per-pass ratio. If people really wanted good numbers then he had those, too. Even up to the middle of this decade Luckman was still rated nineteenth in the all-time list with a 75.0 rating — a mark of his quality.

To tot up such figures in such blood and thunder days is the equivalent of Joe Montana having a Super Bowl season nowadays with only nine men in his offense.

Sid Luckman was the best quarterback ever to work the T-formation and one of the best ever. George 'Papa Bear' Halas said so and that's good enough for anybody.

★★★　Sid Luckman　★★★

Quarterback. 6ft 0in, 195 lb. Born in Brooklyn, New York, 21 November 1916. Attended Columbia University. 1939-50 Chicago Bears.

Passing statistics

Year	Attempts	Completions	Yards	Interceptions	Touchdowns
1939	51	23	636	3	5
1940	105	48	941	9	6
1941	119	68	1,181	6	9
1942	105	57	1,023	13	10
1943	202	110	2,194	12	28
1944	143	71	1,018	11	11
1945	217	117	1,725	10	14
1946	229	110	1,826	16	17
1947	323	176	2,712	31	24
1948	163	89	1,047	14	13
1949	50	22	200	3	1
1950	37	13	180	2	1
Totals	**1744**	**904**	**14,683**	**130**	**139**

Interceptions: 17, 310 yards, 18.2 yard average, 2 touchdowns.
Punting: 230 punts, 8,842 yards, 38.4 yard average, one blocked.

John Madden
The 'A' Type

a coaching career like the brightest shooting star

John Madden had a unique philosophy about head coaches in pro football. He said there were two types. The 'A' type would feel each play on the sideline, hurt after each defeat and worry about each game. Such a coach had a maximum of ten years in his job. The 'B' type, however, were calm on the sidelines, cool about losing and relaxed before the next game. Such a coach could do his job for as long as he wanted.

Madden himself was a classic 'A' type. He would pace the sideline during the game in what appeared to be a blinding rage, afterwards he would be physically drained (particularly after a loss) and he spent too much time before the next game worrying about matters beyond his control.

John Madden was head coach of the Oakland Raiders for exactly ten years.

When Madden took charge of the Raiders in 1969, he was the youngest head coach in pro football at just 32. When he quit in 1979, his record showed an incredible 103 wins, seven ties and only 32 defeats. His tenure at Oakland was an intense affair where he continually asked for more from his team, and usually got it. Such a relatively short period as a head coach had so many triumphs packed into it that Madden's record stands up against the greats without any doubts.

John said when he retired that Don Shula, the colossal head coach at Miami for over twenty years, had been an 'A' type who became a 'B' type. If only Madden himself could have made the same change, his career could have been even more remarkable.

Coaching was something Madden set his heart on from his very earliest days in the game.

He played his college ball at the small California Poly as a useful offensive tackle. As a twenty-first round draft choice of the Philadelphia Eagles, his chances of making a mark as a pro player were remote. A severe knee injury in his first training camp with the

Eagles changed 'remote' to 'impossible'. The injury ended his playing days, yet it also provided him with a basis for his re-directed career as a coach. During his rehabilitation period at the club, Madden spent many hours talking football and watching game film with the Eagles quarterback of the time Norm Van Brocklin.

'That's when I first started learning football,' Madden would recall. Van Brocklin (who himself went on to become an NFL head coach) told his knowledge-hungry rookie teammate that his own coaching method would be to take his best players, find out their best qualities and work the game plan around that. Get maximum use out of the top players and their finest qualities.

With that in mind, Madden got an assistant coaching job at another tiny California college. Two years later he was a head coach with a winning team. He was soon scooped up by the larger organization at San Diego State, a college team run by offensive master Don Coryell.

Coryell (later to gain fame at the NFL's San Diego Chargers) had Madden installed as coach of the defense while he looked after the offense.

The two men were careful to ensure that their respective squads kept pace with each other and, after three hard-driving years, Madden was looking towards his ultimate goal, a head coach's post in the pros.

His penultimate step in that direction came when he was appointed linebacker coach at Oakland in 1967. Raiders owner Al Davis liked his enthusiasm and will to win.

When Davis fell out with his head coach John Rauch two years later, Madden was a surprise choice to replace him. If it was a surprise, it was also a welcome move in the eyes of the players. Madden had no pro playing experience and he was only 32, but the Raiders recognized him as a great teacher and totally dedicated to the task.

Mid-way through his first season, Madden's Raiders met the Buffalo Bills, now coached by his predecessor Rauch. Oakland swamped the Bills 50-21 and Madden's boss announced to the world that his new appointment now had absolute responsibility for the team — something the older, more experienced Rauch had never been given. Al Davis (a former head coach of the year himself) had picked a real winner.

Madden slotted into the Raider organization perfectly. He was

John is now almost as famous for his TV football chalkboard analysis as his years with the Raiders.

more conservative in his play calling than some previous Raider coaches (notably Davis), but the Raider concept of a team pulling together was never better put into practice. In his first seven seasons, Madden's Raiders won six divisional titles, yet in the five times they reached the AFC title game, they lost them all. Was

Madden a flawed head coach?

In reality, his teams had experienced some cruel luck in those title games, particularly the 'Immaculate Reception' play which lost them the 1972 game against Pittsburgh. But Madden wouldn't be denied. In Super Bowl XI he came up with an inspired game plan which crushed Minnesota 32-14. It was the Raider's first world title and it was with Madden's team. The sceptics had been silenced.

If winning the Super Bowl was the end to any 'A' type coach's worries, then Madden had another thing coming. The Raiders only made the play-offs as a wild card team the next season and missed out all together a year later. That was Madden's tenth year in the hot seat. True to his type, he quit before this high pressure job left him drained forever.

As a colour commentator with CBS and on TV in some famous US beer commercials, Madden continued to be in the forefront of football and the public eye.

His image as the coach with the raw emotion and the voice like sandpaper will never fade. The shortness of his head coaching is Madden's only fault: if only he could have found the key to becoming a 'B' type . . .

★★★ **John Madden** ★★★

Head coach. Born in Austin, Minnesota 10 April 1932. Attended California Polytechnic College. 1967-68 assistant coach Oakland Raiders, 1969-78 head coach Oakland Raiders.

Coaching record

Year	Team	Record	Year	Team	Record
1969	Oakland	12-1-1	1975	Oakland	11-3-0
1970	Oakland	8-4-2	1976	Oakland	13-1-0
1971	Oakland	8-4-2	1977	Oakland	11-3-0
1972	Oakland	10-3-1	1978	Oakland	9-7-0
1973	Oakland	9-4-1	**Total**		**103-32-7**
1974	Oakland	12-2-0			

Note: regular season games only

Bronko Nagurski
The Bronk
one of the earliest, the biggest
and the toughest

Some modern football players need statistics to prove their greatness. Bronko Nagurski achieved his elevated status through deeds many and varied, but all of them proving his standing among the gods of the gridiron. It is said that The Bronk was discovered by a college coach who saw him pushing a plough through a field — with no horse! Such a force was harnessed to the great Chicago Bears team of the thirities. Nagurski's contemporaries included the likes of Red Grange and Beattie Feathers, but they are often heard explaining how The Bronk was the best they'd ever seen. After his

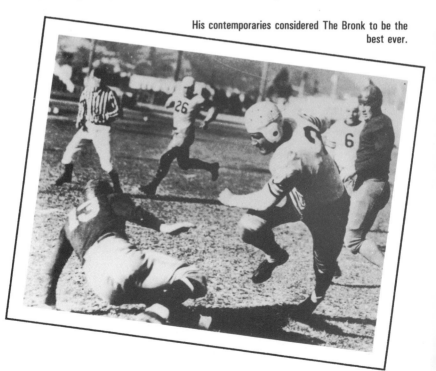

His contemporaries considered The Bronk to be the
best ever.

chance discovery by a coach from University of Minnesota (the coach was actually searching for another potential star), Nagurski was persuaded to use his body for football.

He was actually Canadian, born in a town across a river bordering the land of the Maple Leaf with Minnesota, but he made the move slightly south with ease. His reputation in college ball was big enough to filter down to Chicago where George Halas was building his famed 'Monsters of Midway' team. Nagurski arrived in 1930. The Bears had been pushed back in to the pack of the fledgling NFL. The Bronk soon powered them back to the top.

A backfield containing both him and Grange could hardly *be* contained. In the championship clincher against Portsmouth in 1932, Nagurski showed another side to his talent. Bronko had bulldozed the Bears to within one yeard of the Spartans' goal-line, but was somehow twice beaten back.

On fourth and goal, he was handed the ball again and everyone thought it would be another power play, but instead, Nagurski tossed a short pass to Grange to win the game. He was again on hand for the following year's NFL championship game, the first time two division winners had played in one game for the title. Previously, the title was won on a league basis. Nagurski ran for 65 yards on 14 carries on this historic occasion and, again when the Bears needed it most, he threw a pass which brought the winning touchdown against the New York Giants.

The Bronk actually scored himself a year later in 1934 as his team went for a hat trick of NFL titles. Unfortunately, he was on the losing side and would be again in 1937 when Chicago played in the championship during his 'final' season. That game in '37 was won with the arm of Washington's Sammy Baugh. Nagurski noted that football was changing from the run-orientated game he had grown to love. He decided to retire to take up a career as a wrestler, something else he excelled at.

Nagurski never meant to return to the gridiron, but the Second World War changed his mind. The Bears were still among the greats, but lost many players to the services.

The Bronk made his comeback as tackle at almost 35. As the old magic returned, he moved to fullback. This unstoppable force was instrumental in yet another Bears NFL title. Nagurski had proved just how good an athlete he was and how good a football player, too.

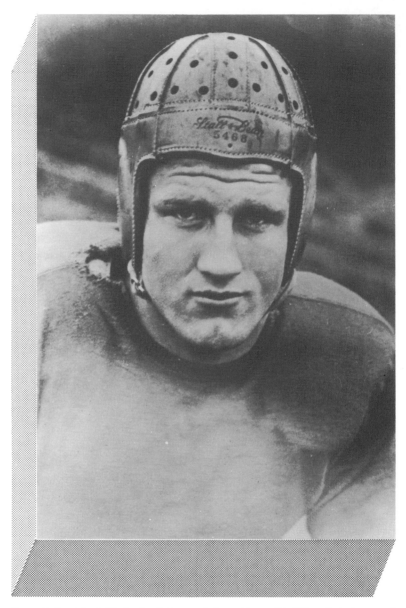

Nagurski played football in the days before statistics could prove his ability — he had to prove it by deeds.

Most of these legendary games were played before statistics became part and parcel of football, so Bronk's unofficial count of 4,031 yards doesn't look too impressive by today's standards. Yet, in the days of the leather helmet and the all-running football games, he had no peer. Nagurski seemed like a house when opponents tried to tackle him — they merely hit him and bounced off again. He hit the tackler as hard as the tackler hit him — an ability he also put to good effect as linebacker on defense.

It's said that, during his peak in the mid-thirities, the owner of the Detroit Lions offered him $10,000 to quit so the Lions could win for a change. A rival coach commented that the only way to stop him was to shoot him before he left the locker room. Such is the legend. His fans recall tall tales of how The Bronk tackled parked cars and horses while others remember how he once crashed into a surrounding wall at Chicago's Wrigley Field stadium — and the crack's still in the wall to prove it!

Believe the tales or not, such recollections prove more than any statistics. Bronko Nagurski made the kind of impression on football that only great players can do — he left memories.

★★★   Bronko Nagurski   ★★★

Fullback. 6ft 2in, 225 lb. Born in Rainy River, Ontario, Canada, 3 November 1908. Attended University of Minnesota. 1930-37, 1943 Chicago Bears.

Rushing statistics Nagurski played football before official records were kept. However, in the NFL annals he's credited with 4,031 career rushing yards in 872 attempts at 4.6 yards per carry.

Joe Namath
Broadway Joe
a legend on and off the field

With one sentence and in one game, Joe Namath became the biggest story in football during the late seventies.

'We'll win Super Bowl III, I guarantee it,' he was quoted as saying. The young quarterback did it, too, and won the heart of a nation at the same time. The remark came before his vulnerable New York Jets took on mighty Baltimore who were favourites by as much as 19 points.

The love of the nation came immediately after Namath guided his men to a shock 16-13 win. The Jets, who represented the fledgling American Football League had finally beaten the monolith that was the National Football League, represented in the big game by the Colts. So the legend of Namath sky-rocketed. He'd beaten the super-strong Colts, he'd beaten the NFL and he'd done it in style after a dose of bravado which could have turned into a millstone.

Namath, of course, had a whole club behind him during Super Bowl III, but his personality was so enormous that few people bother to remember the details. That game was Namath's game — even if he didn't throw a touchdown pass. This incredible young passer had joined the AFL amid controversy, but after a starring college career at Alabama. He was a much-wanted item during the AFL-NFL player war at the time he was drafted.

By chosing the AFL, Namath snubbed the old guard and took a hefty $400,000 contract with New York rather than join the St Louis Cardinals.

The Jets also signed another class rookie in 1965, Heisman Trophy-winning John Huarte. Namath was brought on slowly by Jet's master coach Weeb Ewbank and didn't get the starter's job until half-way through that first season.

He'd had the first of his four knee operations just 23 days after signing, so Ewbank's move was a sensible one. With Namath at the helm, the Jets' fortunes began to look up.

Joe would pass for over 3,000 yards in three of his first four years

Namath's greatest season with the Jets for statistics was '67 when he became the first passer to top the 4,000 yards mark.

126

Broadway Joe had the good looks which attracted women to watch the game.

— a period which ended with the Super Bowl win.

The sort of Namath day the fans longed for each week was, perhaps, typified by a career-best 496 yards and six touchdowns performance against the unlucky Baltimore a few seasons after the Big Game loss.

Such pass-ability had brought him the honour of being the first 4,000-yard passer pro football history back in 1967.

The hype which accompanied his career during these glory days was immense. Namath was photographed dating actresses like Raquel Welch, he starred in a movie with Ann Margaret, he lived in a lavish penthouse with six-inch deep rugs of llama fur, slept in a gigantic oval bed and strolled around the hottest nightspots in a

$5,000 mink overcoat. He even owned his own club which had to close amid more controversy.

Namath had the presence of a movie star.' He had the same electrifying qualities I found in Clark Gable, Gregory Peck, Joan Crawford and Marilyn Monroe,' said Jets owner and showbiz agent Sonny Werblin who is said to have covered the cost of Joe's original contract in just one week of ticket sales.

That was the pulling power of Namath. That man who models a line of underpants, talks about his sex life rather than football and walks with a wolfish swagger like Namath's had playboy potential to match his playing potential. By 1972, Joe's annual salary of $250,000 made him the highest paid player in the league, but by now his knees were beginning to show signs of wear and tear. Knee braces were put on both knees, but he'd be missing from action for many games. His reputation was carrying him through, even though his career was declining.

After a poor 1976 (both personally and for the team), Namath was traded to the Los Angeles Rams. He played only six more games, retiring after four interceptions on a Monday night game watched by a coast-to-coast TV audience. His off-the-field persona was large enough to keep him in the football and public eye. He even had one season as a colour commentator on the very Monday Night Football programme which saw the end of his career.

Namath has truly done it all. 'The greatest athlete I've ever coached,' his Alabama mentor Paul 'Bear' Bryant called him. He was AFL rookie of the year in '65. He was Super Bowl III Most Valuable Player. He was the first recipient of the George Halas Award for the Most Courageous Pro Player. The Jets retired his no 12 shirt in 1985. He'd already joined the ranks of the Hall of Fame. The fox really had learned to run with the hounds. The NFL, which must have winced at Namath's playboy style and his effect on their league and image, had accepted his role in the history of football.

The Namath Super Bowl was the one which caught the American public's imaginiation. The brash Pennsylvanian quarterback was the reason why. That day in early 1969, Joe Namath didn't just win a football game. He didn't just legitimize a football league. He helped lasso the public to follow the whole sport of football.

The man with the wild-boy image, the dark good looks and the many different women on his arm was a guy everyone could relate to.

Above There were more downs than ups over the years with the Jets — only three winning seasons.
Right On the sideline at Super Bowl III, Namath wonders about his guaranteed victory.

America really fell in love with two men when it took the Jets quarterback to its heart — Joe Namath the football player and Joe Namath the man.

★★★ **Joe Namath** ★★★

Quarterback. 6ft 2in, 200 lb. Born in Beaver Falls, Pennsylvania, 31 May 1943. Attended Alabama University. 1965-76 New York Jets. 1977 Los Angeles Rams.

Passing statistics

Year	Games	Attempts	Completions	Percentage passes completed	Yards	Touchdowns	Interceptions
+ 1965	14	340	164	48.2	2220	18	15
+ 1966	14	471	232	49.3	3379	19	27
+ 1967	14	491	258	52.5	40007	26	28
+ 1968	14	380	187	49.2	3147	15	17
+ 1969	14	361	185	51.2	2734	19	17
+ 1970	5	179	90	50.3	1259	5	12
+ 1971	4	59	28	47.5	537	5	6
+ 1972	13	324	162	50.0	2816	19	21
+ 1973	6	133	68	51.1	966	5	6
+ 1974	14	361	191	52.9	2616	20	22
+ 1975	14	326	157	48.2	2286	15	28
+ 1976	11	230	114	49.6	1090	4	16
* 1977	6	107	50	46.7	606	3	5
Totals	**143**	**3,762**	**1,886**	**50.1**	**27,663**	**173**	**220**

+ with New York Jets
* with Los Angeles Rams

Rushing: 71 carries, 140 yards, 2.0 average, 7 touchdowns.

Pete Pihos
The Golden Greek
the term 'impact player' fitted him perfectly

Back in the 1940s, no one talked about 'impact' players. The term hadn't been coined in time for Pete Pihos, but it would have fitted him perfectly.

The experts knew Pihos had a large chunk of greatness in him before he even pulled on his cleats in the pro game. He was drafted third overall by Philadelphia in 1945 even though the Eagles knew he had to spend two years in the army. 'I can wait for a player like Pihos,' said coach Earl (Greasy) Neale.

When Pihos did arrive his effect was immediate — the Eagles went straight to the NFL championship game. Philadelphia had drafted him after his exploits at Indiana University at fullback but the Eagles already had a great player in that position — Steve Van Buren, another man destined for the Hall of Fame. So Coach Neale put the Indiana star at right end and devised the Pihos screen — a short pass play behind the line of scrimmage to Pihos who then used his fullback abilities to blast upfield.

The plan worked up until that first title game in 1947 which the Eagles lost 28-21 to the Chicago Cardinals. But they got revenge a year later against the same club (a 7-0 win) with Pihos in the thick of the action. Pihos' success continued when he caught the opening touchdown pass in the 1949 NFL championship game against the LA Rams to give the Eagles their second NFL title.

So, after just three years in the league, Pihos had been to three title games in the NFL and won twice. Yet he wasn't renowned as a speedster. Instead he caught his passes because of an absolute determination. By now Pihos had used that skill to replace Green Bay's Don Hutson as the greatest pass receiver in the league.

Like Hutson, Pihos could also play defense — and how. He'd caught 176 passes for the Eagles in his first five seasons while he played both offense and defense and during this time he won the honour of being named in the all-NFL team as an end.

But in 1952 Philadelphia had a spate of injuries which changed

Above This is the sort of difficult catch that a great player like Pihos could make look easy.
Left Pete Pihos was predicted to reach greatness with Philadelphia after a great college career.

Pihos' role. The versatile Pete Pihos turned into a full-time defensive end for a year and performed with such distinction that he was then named in the all-NFL team for his play on defense.

The following season Pihos took his 6 ft 1 in, 210 lb frame back over to the offense and had the first of three great years. From 1953 to 1955 he caught 63, 60 and 62 passes — fabulous totals for a man who played both ways and in the days when football was still mainly a running game.

He had managed to cash in on his ability when he started as a pro (he signed a contract for $17,000 in 1947) and was able to retire in 1955 at the pinnacle of his career.

Pihos had just won three consecutive NFL passing titles by then and capped it all with a memorable game in the 1956 Pro Bowl. It was the sixth time he'd played in the annual fixture for the best NFL players and it was to be his final game.

Pihos' career record finished at 373 catches for 5,619 yards and 378 points. Those figures were the reason why he was named in the All-Pro squad for the entire 1940s decade and later, in 1970, enshrined into the Hall of Fame.

The man they called 'the Golden Greek' (his ancestors had come to America from Greece) was one of those special players who had the build, speed and brain to be an outstanding sixty-minute football player. In nine years as a pro he missed just one game and struck fear into the hearts of defenders who tried to stop him catching passes and opposing yard-gainers who tried to get past him.

Perhaps the most-fitting compliment about Pihos came from his coach at Philadelphia during his final four seasons, Jim Trimble. 'He's the best all-round end in the league', said Trimble, 'and I wish I had half a dozen like him.' Having Pete Pihos in your team was almost as good as having an extra six men anyway.

★★★   Pete Pihos   ★★★

End. 6ft 1in, 210 lb. Born in Orlando, Florida on 22 October 1923. Attended Indiana University. 1947-55 Philadelphia Eagles.

Receiving statistics

Year	Receipts	Yards	Average	Touchdowns
1947	23	382	16.6	7
1948	46	766	16.7	11
1949	34	484	14.2	4
1950	38	447	11.8	6
1951	35	536	15.3	5
1952	12	219	18.3	1
1953	63	1,049	16.7	10
1954	60	872	14.5	10
1955	62	864	13.9	7
Total	373	5,619	15.1	61

John Riggins
The Diesel
the top exponent of Rigginomics

A diesel needs plenty of fuel to keep on truckin'. John Riggins' nickname was 'The Diesel' and his fuel was to carry the football. The more he got the ball, the more he liked it and the more damage he would do.

But there was much more to this unconventional anti-hero. The man who once sported a Mohican hairstyle with gold earring, who quit for a year to take up farming, who won Super Bowl XVIII — John Riggins was all these things. Riggo seemed to get better as he got older and as he found a coach who knew how to handle him and how to use him.

He became one of that select group of men to run for more than 10,000 yards during his career. It was mostly done by the sort of power running that could break lesser men in half. Riggins actually got out of his hospital bed to gain some of it. His sort of running needed that sort of bravery.

Riggins was a bull of a runner at the University of Kansas and his efforts (which included breaking records set by that phenomenal broken-field runner Gayle Sayers) prompted the New York Jets to make him the sixth man taken in the entire 1971 draft.

The Jets had won the Super Bowl three seasons earlier, but were now tail-spinning into obscurity. They were still Namath's team, Broadway Joe Namath, that film star-style footballer. The fact that Riggins actually gained some notices while in the shade of such a large gridiron personality is testimony to his ability.

The farm boy from Middle America seemed to excel despite the hype of New York and its preoccupation with his team's quarterback. In his rookie year, Riggins led the team in both rushing and receiving.

Over the next four seasons he was one of the Jets' mainstays. By 1975 he had his first 1,000-yard rushing season (the first Jet ever to achieve this). Those were the days of some of his most outrageous behaviour — notably the Mohican cut, the gold chains and the

Riggins became the Jets' first-ever 1,000 yard rusher in 1975.

hippy sunglasses.

But it was his final year at the Jets. The lure of a $1½ million contract with Washington was enough to give them yet another free agent in Riggins.

Redskins coach at the time, George Allen, had already constructed one Super Bowl team out of free agents and cast-offs and thought he could build another.

Unfortunately, Allen never stayed to see the best of his signing from the Jets. Riggins seemed a little bemused by a new team in his first year and was injured for much of the second. After that, Allen left to coach the LA Rams.

The Diesel got rolling over the next two seasons which were both thousand-yarders, but trouble was on the way. Riggins was

Riggins taking hand-offs from Redskins quarterback Joe
Theismann became one of the sweetest sights in football in the eighties.

suspended in the '79 training camp for missing practice and almost
retired there and then. However, negotiations for his contract
renewal broke down after the season finished. Riggins sat out the
entire 1980 season and used the time to grow corn on his Kansas
farm.

The following season, the Redskins appointed another new
coach, Joe Gibbs from San Diego. Gibbs had the reputation for
extravagant passing offenses, yet he knew how important a
possessional fullback like John Riggins would be to his plans. Gibbs
actually went to Riggins' farm in person to persuade him to give up
his hermit-like existence and play ball. Riggins agreed and history
was soon being written in a big way.

The '81 season saw the Redskins and Gibbs undergoing a

Left There have been few more effective fullbacks from inside the five-yard line than The Diesel.

★

Right The Diesel is shot here during his MVP-winning performance against Miami in Super Bowl XIX.

settling-in-period. The following year would be theirs. The season was shortened by the players' strike, but Washington finished on top of the NFC's restructured sixteen-team table. Riggins was a steady ground-gainer, but in the play-offs he exploded. In three games he barrelled for 119, 185 and 140 yards. In Super Bowl XVII, he had a mammoth game, 166 yards (then a Super Bowl record) and the game-busting TD when he got round left end for a 43-yard run to glory.

'Rigginomics' is what the game's MVP citation dubbed the tactic in honour of incumbent President Reagan's economic policy. Riggins had actually demanded the ball 25 or 30 times a match. He reckoned that would win the game — and he was right.

The truck rolled on in '83 with Riggins' best-ever season, 1,347 yards and an NFL record 24 TDs. By now, the one-back formation which starred Riggins in a lonely Redskin backfield was turning into

an NFL craze.

Opponents knew he'd get the ball (especially in goalline plays) and they knew he'd probably thunder over the left side of Washington's monster-sized offensive line (nicknamed 'The Hogs'), but they still couldn't stop him. Riggins cleared the path to another Super Bowl in 1983. However, it would be the LA Raiders' day. They scored early and plenty. The Riggins style wasn't meant for quick catch-up situations and he was held to a miserly 64 yards and one TD.

In '84, a niggling back injury meant Riggins was in a hospital bed almost as often as in training. Age was catching him up. The following season he saw only limited action as Coach Gibbs looked to a successor. The Diesel had finally broken down.

Amidst all the awards Riggins received, he was probably most surprised to be the first gridiron superstar of the British football public. His game-clinching run in Super Bowl XVII capped a first season of football on British TV screens. He was their hero as well as America's.

It's the sort of crazy thing that would appeal to a man like John Riggins.

★★★ John Riggins ★★★

Fullback. 6ft 2in, 240 lb. Born in Centralia, Kansas on 4 August 1949. Attended University of Kansas. 1971-75 New York Jets, 1976-85 Washington Redskins.

Rushing statistics

Year	Rushes	Yards	Average	Touchdowns
* 1971	180	769	4.3	1
* 1972	207	944	4.6	7
* 1973	134	482	3.6	4
* 1974	169	680	4.0	5
* 1975	238	1005	4.2	8
+ 1976	162	572	3.5	3
+ 1977	68	203	3.0	0
+ 1978	248	1014	4.1	5
+ 1979	260	1153	4.4	9
+ 1981	195	714	3.7	13
+ 1982	177	553	3.1	3
+ 1983	375	1347	3.6	24
+ 1984	327	1239	3.8	14
+ 1985	176	677	3.8	8
Totals	**2,916**	**11,452**	**3.9**	**104**

* with NY Jets
+ with Washington

Receiving: 250 catches, 2,094 yards, 8.4 yard average, 12 touchdowns.

Jim Ringo
Centre Point

the hub of one of the greatest teams

There is no position on the gridiron that is more unheralded than that of the centre. Of the entire offensive line, the centre seems to take the most knocks with the least credit.

Yet, the great centres need many superb qualities — toughness, cunning, longevity and bravery among them. A player like Jim Ringo had all those qualities and more.

Ringo was one of the major reasons why the Green Bay Packers were a great side in the sixties. Every era team needs a hub to mould itself around and Ringo was that for the Pack. He would play through their winning years despite injury and pain, but would always give a special effort for his team's sake. That kind of dedication might not bring fan adulation like the 'skill' positions, but respect from his fellow professionals meant a lot to Jim Ringo.

Ringo was the man about whom Coach Lombardi built his Green Bay offense.

There were several things that made Ringo's career an even more remarkable one. Firstly, he was a relatively small man to play in such a position. Just 6ft 1in and a mere 220 lb (in his heyday) meant that Ringo never had a bulk advantage over the marauding defensive lineman who were after his quarterback. Secondly, Ringo suffered a series of illnesses during his fifteen seasons that should have laid him low for many a long day. There were severe infections, boils, a severely strained back (initially diagnosed as a broken back), pneumonia and gammy knees. These problems didn't prevent him starting 182 consecutive games in the NFL — which was a record in 1967.

Such a run wouldn't have been predicted at the start of the Ringo career fifteen seasons earlier in 1953. The young centre had just survived a 61-5 thrashing with Syracuse University in the Rose Bowl when he was drafted in the seventh round by the Packers. The difference between the homely atmosphere of Syracuse and the hard-nosed all-out-win attitude of the pros left him a little bemused.

He walked out of his first training camp with the Packers because he felt unable to compete with the giants who were also trying out for the centre's position. Neither did he like the military style of coaching imposed by Gene Ronzani, but his family persuaded him to at least give it a chance and Ringo soon impressed with his powerful blocking and fine technique. He didn't have the bulk, but he had the brains and used them to immediately claim the starter's job.

However, Ringo's good work couldn't lift Green Bay out of the doldrums. They had become confirmed losers. But, in 1959, a new coach arrived who would change the team, change the won-loss column and change Ringo's fortunes, as well.

That man was Vince Lombardi and the new coach paid a huge tribute to his starting centre who was the only man on the team who had won All Pro status. Indeed, he built the Packers offense around the hard-working Ringo.

Lombardi installed a relentless rushing game which would feature his linemen 'pulling' to lead-block for his runningbacks. Ringo became a master at this tactic. His lightness allowed him tremendous mobility which meant the Packers favourite sweep plays featured the sledgehammer of Ringo at their head.

Suddenly, Ringo was playing on a winning team and he was in charge of the offensive line — the Packer's key to consistent victory.

The classic centre's position — Ringo gets ready to snap to Packers' QB Bart Starr.

He would make the calls for line blocking on downs and always seemed to be on hand to help a fellow lineman who was under pressure as they formed a pass pocket for quarterback Bart Starr. Ringo played in three consecutive NFL title games, winning two and losing one, between 1960 and 62.

In 1963, after eleven years with the Pack, Ringo fell out with his mentor, Coach Lombardi. The eleven-year centre had taken an agent with him to discuss more money on a new contract. The ebullient Lombardi didn't like the look of an agent meddling with these matters (something which is commonplace nowadays) and traded Ringo to Philadelphia.

The Eagles were in decline and had just finished bottom of their division. By Ringo's final season, four years later, Philadelphia had achieved a respectable third. He'd helped construct their offensive line too, so often the key to NFL success.

It's been estimated that Ringo must have snapped the ball to quarterbacks, punters or placekick holders (he did all the snapping jobs) more than 12,000 times.

It's also been estimated that the number of bad snaps he gave was less than a handfull.

No one doubts either of these estimates.

★★★   Jim Ringo   ★★★

Centre. 6ft 1in, 235 lb. Born in Orange, New Jersey, 21 November, 1932. Attended Syracuse University. 1953-1963 Green Bay Packers, 1964-67 Philadelphia Eagles.

Gayle Sayers
Shooting Star
his star rose fast and high

The average career for an NFL player has been estimated at about $4\frac{1}{2}$ years. Injury, loss of form or competition from other players are the causes of a man being cut from the team. And of those three factors, injury is the hardest one for any man to swallow. It's especially difficult to take when the physical rigours of the NFL cut short an amazing talent. Gayle Sayers was such a talent.

No loss of form affected him. No competition for his runningback spot was too fierce. The only cut that Sayers ever suffered was from the surgeon's knife. The heavy-duty blows to Sayers' right knee reduced his actual playing time to little more than the $4\frac{1}{2}$-year average. But no one has achieved so much in such a short time. Sayers didn't just take the league by the scruff of the neck, he picked it up and threw it around as well.

The 6ft 0in, 200 lb jazz-loving student from Kansas University was drafted by the Chicago Bears in the first round in 1965. Sayers then proceeded to re-write page after page of the NFL record book. As unanimous rookie of the year he amassed an unprecedented 132 points, scored 22 touchdowns and left the football world open-mouthed.

In one match against the New York Giants, Sayers had a wonder game. He rushed for 113 yards in nine carries, got 89 more yards on two pass receptions and 134 on five punt returns. A total of 336 yards on only sixteen plays. Just one week later against the San Francisco 49ers he became only the third man in NFL history to score six touchdowns in one game.

His second season showed no let-up. His first 1,000-yard year, a combined 2,440 yardage mark and a second Pro Bowl appearance. In 1967 the honours and the achievements piled high again, but then came the hurt. Sayers took one blow too many to his right knee after only nine games of the following season. His whole career was in doubt.

It then required another kind of courage from this remarkable

The silky running of Sayers was only actually on show for a total of $4\frac{1}{2}$ seasons.

athlete. And he proved he had it by fighting back to the top of his profession. In 1969 he was back and rushed for 1,032 yards to return to the Pro Bowl for the fourth time.

The sport bestowed on him the George Halas Trophy as the most courageous player of the year. But, typical of the man, Sayers gave the award away. He passed it on to his close friend and fellow

Sayers became one of only a handful of men to score six touchdowns in a single game.

Chicago Bear Brian Piccolo who was dying of cancer. This outstanding gesture of honour became part of football folklore and was later immortalized in a film called *Brian's Song*. But awards and ceremonies were soon replaced by more hospital appointments for Sayers. He struggled through just two games in the 1970 season and only two more the following year.

Both knees had now been operated on and the word 'comeback' was continually mentioned next to his name. In 1972 he would try one final time. Careful rehabilitation and supervized training were employed but it was all for nothing — his football days were over.

The Bears during the Sayers days were not up among the contenders. Their graceful halfback was one of their few real class acts, but he was never offered the same standard of protection. It's another tribute to him that he triumphed despite it all. If Gayle Sayers had stayed healthy longer, there is no knowing what he would have achieved. His NFL days were short, but those who saw him play were honoured to do so.

He was really a victim of his own success. As a broken-field runner, he had no equal. His kick-off return average of over thirty yards per carry is the sort of figure that is almost unimaginable. Sayers was so outstanding that the Bears *had* to use him on returns because he was such a threat. Yet, it's on special teams that the football athletes take the heaviest beatings. Bodies hitting head-on at full speed often carry the worst risk of injury. Special team play and gridiron longevity don't mix.

Sayers had run like a wildcat past bamboozled defenders in a short sprint lined with glory. He had dodged and weaved through the smallest of gaps. He had made his own limelight. He was a star in public while in private he was a devoted and affectionate friend. That star had risen high and fast. Its descent had been both tragic and premature.

★★★ Gayle Sayers ★★★

Runningback. 6ft 0in, 200 lb. Born in Wichita, Kansas, 30 May 1943. Attended Kansas University. 1965-71 Chicago Bears.

Rushing statistics

Year	Games	Attempts	Yards	Average	Touchdowns
1965	14	166	867	5.2	14
1966	14	229	1,231	5.4	8
1967	13	186	830	4.7	7
1968	9	138	856	6.2	2
1969	14	236	1,032	4.4	8
1970	2	23	52	2.3	0
1971	2	13	38	2.9	0
Total	68	991	4,956	5.0	39

Punt returns: 28, 391 yards, 14.0 yard average, 2 touchdowns.
Kick-off returns: 91, 2,781 yards, 30.6 yard average, 6 touchdowns.

O. J. Simpson
The Juice
flowed majestically into the history books

Orenthal James Simpson doesn't sound like the name of a football phenomenon. 'The Juice' has a sweeter ring to it. The name brings to mind one of the most beautiful sights in the whole of sport — an uninhibited talent running free on a football field.

O. J. Simpson had a natural talent for the gridiron game. He seemed to go from nought to top speed quicker than a rocket; he burst through holes almost before they appeared and he had enough moves to fool entire defenses let alone one would-be tackler.

Yet, as a child, those legs that would rack up the records needed braces to support them. Luckily, the young O.J., as he was usually known, had a great desire to rise out of his poor background. His boyhood hero was Cleveland's living legend Jim Brown. By chance

The Juice's greatest hour was in 1973 when he became the first runningback to crack the 2,000 yard barrier in one season.

At University of Southern California, the world first saw Simpson's famous no 32 cut through defenses.

the thirteen-year-old O.J. met his hero in a San Francisco ice cream parlour. 'You ain't so tough,' he told Brown, 'Someday I'm gonna break all your records.' He nearly did, too.

There was no doubt during four wonderful years at University of Southern California that O.J. would be challenging for Brown's mantle as the greatest-ever.

But after the 1969 draft there was a doubt. Simpson had won the Heisman Trophy and had hoped for a West Coast team to pick him up. However, the draft says the worst pick first and Buffalo were undoubtedly the worst.

Snow-covered fields in Buffalo were too much of a contrast from sunshine fields of California at first. Simpson baulked. He asked for $500,000 a year. He got $50,000 as Bills' owner Ralph Wilson dug his heels in. O.J. signed reluctantly and made up the financial difference by signing lucrative endorsements.

The trouble didn't end there. Bills coach John Rauch and O.J. were at war from the start. Simpson hardly got the ball in Rauch's

It's hard to believe that such a super athlete needed braces on his legs as a child.

game plan and was more often used as decoy or receiver than ball carrier. The doubts began. Three wasted years left him disillusioned, but a saviour arrived in new coach Lou Saban who built Buffalo's entire offense around The Juice. Saban gathered offensive linemen who could open up holes for his star and made sure O.J. got plenty of the pigskin. The days of Rauch suddenly seemed like a nightmare.

The first season with Saban in control ended with Simpson as NFL rushing champion with 1,251 yards. The team itself won only four games, but O.J. knew his hour had arrived. The following year it happened. Simpson opened his season with an NFL record 250 yards rushing against New England. He would go on to finish his season with another record, the type that might never be beaten — 2,000 yards in only fourteen games.

With thirteen of the fourteen regular season matches over, Simpson had amassed 1,803 yards. That magical number of 2,000 yards in a season had never been achieved. Did O.J. have a chance to do it? The Bills' final match of the year was against the New York Jets on a frozen, snowy pitch at Shea Stadium. Those doubts began again. But not even the elements could stop O.J. on that day of destiny. The record-breaking run was a seven-yarder behind his left guard and no 1 blocker Reggie McKenzie. O.J. had done the impossible: 2,003 yards.

There were still almost six minutes left in the game, but no one cared as The Juice was carried shoulder-high from the field. In that one season he'd set eight NFL rushing records and made Buffalo the first team in the league to rush for 3,000 yards in a season.

Even with this supreme effort, the Bills missed the play-offs. They did manage it a year later in '74 as a wild card, but O.J. had badly damaged his right ankle in the first game of the season and the hurting never really let up, yet he still managed a 1,000 yard season.

In the play-off opener, Buffalo lost 32-14 to mighty Pittsburgh. O.J. did score one touchdown, but was held to 77 yards rushing. It would be his only experience of NFL play-offs.

In 1976 Simpson seemed to give it one last shot. Individual glory had quenched his appetite for a while, but he wanted team glory. He wanted a Super Bowl.

The Juice ran wild for 1,817 yards only to see the Bills defense play Santa Claus each week. Buffalo could do no better than an 8-6 mark and dropped to third place in their division. O.J.'s frustrations came to the surface. He tried to hold out for a trade to the West Coast where his family still lived. Owner Wilson again held firm. Simpson eventually signed for a huge $2.2 million, but his spirit seemed broken.

Fans booed when he turned up out of shape for the '76 opener. He showed some sparkle (notably a 273-yard day against Detroit) and made it to second place in the all-time rushing list behind boyhood hero Jim Brown. Simpson passed another landmark the next year, the 10,000-yard career rushing barrier, but was out for half the season after knee surgery.

Finally, in 1978, he got his wish for a trade. San Francisco, his home-town team signed him up. The Juice had come home at last. However, the 49ers at that time were even worse than Buffalo. His career was virtually over. It lasted through the '79 campaign before

Simpson's achievements are more remarkable when you consider that he played so many games on the snow-covered home pitch at Buffalo.

he took up a job as a football commentator on TV and dabbled in movies. His credits would include *Towering Inferno* and *Capricorn One.*

In Buffalo, Simpson's offensive line was named 'The Electric Company' for it was they who 'turned on' The Juice. How dissatisfying that they couldn't offer one outstanding individual just one outstanding team season. O.J. Simpson was indeed an electric runner. In college he was part of a 4 × 400 metre relay team that broke a world athletics record. If he'd been carrying a football rather than a baton, maybe he'd have run even faster.

★★★ O.J. Simpson ★★★

Runningback. 6ft 1in, 212 lb. Born in San Francisco, California, on 9 July 1947. Attended University of Southern California. 1969-77 Buffalo Bills, 1978-79 San Francisco 49ers.

Rushing statistics

Year	Games	Attempts	Yards	Average	Touchdowns
+ 1969	13	181	697	3.9	2
+ 1970	8	120	488	4.1	5
+ 1971	14	183	742	4.1	5
+ 1972	14	292	1,251	4.3	6
+ 1973	14	332	2,003	6.0	12
+ 1974	14	270	1,125	4.2	3
+ 1975	14	329	1,817	5.5	16
+ 1976	14	290	1,503	5.2	8
+ 1977	7	126	557	4.4	0
* 1978	10	161	593	3.7	1
* 1979	13	120	460	3.8	3
Total	**135**	**2,404**	**11,236**	**4.7**	**61**

+ with Buffalo Bills
* with San Francisco 49ers

Receiving: 203 catches, 2,142 yards, 10.6 yard average, 14 touchdowns.

Passing: 16 attempts, 6 completions, 37.5 percentage passes completed, 110 yards, 1 touchdown.

Kick-off returns: 33, 990 yards, 30.0 yard average, 1 touchdown.

Ken Stabler
The Snake
probably the best leftie of all-time

Style doesn't count for everything on the gridiron. Not when it can be replaced by winning. If a guy gets the job done, then that's what counts. Ken Stabler was such a player. He admitted himself that there were many better quarterbacks in the league when it came to passing style, but there were few better quarterbacks when it came to leading a team, few better motivators. In short, Stabler was a winner. He had a typical quarterback's swagger. He knew what it took to get the job done and had the self-confidence to carry it out.

There have been few left-handed QBs that have made an impression on the game and Stabler was undoubtedly the best of them. 'Lefties' as left-handed QBs are called in America are unusual — but then Ken Stabler was an unusual player.

His college career touched the highest standards. He played under the great Paul 'Bear' Bryant at Alabama where he performed

★ ★ ★

Snake Stabler wasn't always a pure stylist, but he invariably got the job done.

★ ★ ★

Here in Super Bowl XI, Stabler drops back to
get Oakland moving to Victory.

in three of the four major bowls, the Sugar, Orange and Cotton. In '65, Stabler led the Crimson Tide to a national championship with a perfect 11-0 record.

He was picked up in the second round of the '68 draft by the Oakland Raiders, but they already had George Blanda and Daryle Lamonica in the passing position.

Stabler was farmed out to a semi-pro team called the Spokane Shockers for a couple of seasons' experience and didn't throw a pass in the NFL until 1970. His game time slowly increased over the next two seasons until he unseated Lamonica for the starting QB job after three games of the '73 campaign. Stabler went on to make the Pro Bowl.

The Raiders' new leader maintained their challenge for honours by guiding them into the AFC title game where only reigning Super Bowl champions Miami proved too strong.

This outstanding beginning confirmed Stabler as the Raiders QB and he proved his worth in the next season as he tossed 26 touchdowns on the way to becoming AFC player of the year. In that year's AFC title game, Stabler racked up 249 yards in passing compared to just 95 by his opposite number, Terry Bradshaw of Pittsburgh — yet the Raiders lost 24-13. However, Stabler made his second consecutive Pro Bowl appearance.

The emerging Steelers performed the same feat on Stabler's Raiders in '75 as Ken began to have trouble with too many interceptions (24 against only sixteen touchdowns).

However, 1976 proved that Stabler still knew how to win. Oakland again won their division (the fifth year running and the fourth with Ken at the helm) and Stabler starred in the play-offs. He scored the winning TD on a one-yard run as time expired against New England and threw two TD passes as the Raiders slipped past Pittsburgh.

So onto Super Bowl XI against Minnesota. Now the Raiders had the reputation as the sport's bad boys and had yet to win this ultimate trophy. Stabler led them to an overwhelming victory. Ken's pass rating for that season was a wonderful 103.7 and in the Super Bowl he led long drive after long drive, throwing one TD himself early in the game.

In '77, Stabler got interception fever again. In one game against Denver, he was picked off seven times. The Broncos ultimately stopped Oakland returning to the Super Bowl. Stabler threw two TDs in that title game, but Denver won 20-17.

In the next two seasons, Stabler went pass crazy. There were 406 attempts in '78 and an incredible 498 in '79 as the whole Raiders team took a slump. Ken's arm was questioned (it threw thirty interceptions in '78) and eventually he was traded to Houston for the start of the 1980 season.

The Oilers were fresh from two wild card play-off years — Stabler wouldn't let them down. Ironically it was Oakland who would beat them in 1980 and went on to win the Super Bowl. The defeat was particularly hard on Stabler who had two disasterous interceptions — one in Oakland's end zone and the second run back for a touchdown.

He lasted just one more season at Houston before signing as a free agent with New Orleans to play under Coach Bum Phillips who'd been fired by the Oilers after the 1980 Oakland defeat. Phillips recognized Stabler as a man who could give the Saints the best chance of their first-ever winning season. At that time, Ken was the most accurate passer in NFL history with 60.3 percent completion rate.

Stabler finished off his career at New Orleans — a team he nearly led to their first ever winning season.

Stabler's Saints missed out in the '82 strike season, but then went as close as they'd ever been in '83 as the old hand guided the wheel with tremendous panache. He made the most of limited resources and New Orleans needed to beat the LA Rams in their final game to get a wild card. On the third play of the third quarter Stabler was hit hard. His pass was intercepted and was returned for a Rams touchdown. He left the field for good and the Saints lost..

There wasn't much left to his career after that. Age and injuries had taken their toll and Stabler retired during the '84 season when he felt he could no longer do a good job at New Orleans. He was nearing 40 years old.

Stabler was a maverick kind of player who finished his career among the all-time highest-rated passers and with a reputation as a winner. His attitude to the game was summed up in one of his quotes. 'Winning is what we're all here for. It cures colds, heals fever blisters, whatever's wrong with you . . . I can make guys win. I can motivate players and they'll tell you that. It's part of my job.'

★★★   Ken Stabler   ★★★

Quarterback. 6ft 3in, 210 lb. Born in Foley, Alabama, on 25 December 1945. Attended University of Alabama. 1970-79 Oakland Raiders, 1980-81 Houston Oilers, 1982-84 New Orleans Saints.

Passing statistics

Year	Attempts	Completions	Yards	Touchdowns	Interceptions
+ 1970	7	2	52	0	1
+ 1971	48	24	268	1	4
+ 1972	74	44	524	4	3
+ 1973	260	163	1997	14	10
+ 1974	310	178	2469	26	12
+ 1975	293	171	2296	16	24
+ 1976	291	194	2737	27	17
+ 1977	294	169	2176	20	20
+ 1978	406	237	2944	16	30
+ 1979	498	304	3615	26	22
● 1980	457	293	3202	13	28
● 1981	285	165	1988	14	18
* 1982	189	117	1343	6	10
* 1983	311	176	1988	9	18
* 1984	70	33	339	2	5
Total	3,793	2,270	27,938	194	222

+ with Oakland Raiders
● with Houston Oilers
* with New Orleans Saints

Bart Starr
Super Starr

was the sixties' most incomparable field lieutenant

When you're a seventeenth round draft choice in the NFL, then there's not much chance of you making the squad. You certainly won't get a starting job and don't expect to get into any Pro Bowl teams or awards of any kind. If that's the height of low-round draft choice's expectations, how come Bart Starr achieved all that and more? How come he played for sixteen years, won five NFL titles, two Super Bowls (in both those matches he was MVP), played in four Pro Bowls and was voted NFL player of the year in 1966?

For three pro seasons, none of those glorious triumphs looked even remotely possible. Starr had performed admirably at Alabama University where coaches claimed he was the best ever passer from this illustrious football factory. However, Bart didn't share their

★

Starr defied considerable odds to make the grade as a pro — he was a seventeenth round draft pick.

★

confidence in him. Once in the pros, Starr seemed like just another rookie. He got a little playing time, but didn't look like the Packers' answer to a true field General. They needed such a player because they were going through a relatively thin time as far as results were concerned.

Green Bay had been living among the best in the thirties and forties, so their poor form in the fifties needed to be reversed. No one knew that Starr would play such a big part in that revival until coach Vince Lombardi arrived in 1959.

Starr's job was actually on the line at this time, yet Lombardi saw something in his manner and style which he liked. The coach particularly admired his intelligence.

Lombardi didn't load the Packers' full QB responsibilities on Starr immediately, not until his confidence had been built up. That had happened by 1960, when Bart was No 1 quarterback in his fitth season. It also happened to mark the return of Green Bay to the title trail. A divisional title got the Packers into the NFL championship game, but they lost 17-13 to Philadelphia despite Bart out-performing Eagles famed QB Norm Van Brocklin.

The following season, three Starr passes found their targets for touchdowns as the Pack won the NFL title with a 37-0 win over the New York Giants. It was the start of one of the most dominant eras in pro football and Bart Starr was at the centre of it.

A second title followed immediately in 1962 and a third in 1965. Starr and his mentor, Lombardi, were a familiar sight by now on the Packers sideline. The two men would decide on the battle plan and the quarterback would execute it to perfection.

Green Bay's assault on every NFL title at that time was based on a balanced offense. It didn't always give a chance for Starr's personal effort to stand out, but there would be no doubt as to his contribution after the next two seasons.

The NFL-AFL merger had just been signed and a Super Bowl (although it wasn't called that at the time) was the prize for all to fight for.

Starr guided the Pack past Dallas to win the NFL with a masterful show, four touchdown passes and 304 yards. Then on they went to meet Kansas City in what would later be called Super Bowl I.

Field Marshal Starr threw two more TDs as Green Bay won easily and he was voted MVP — the next season, the Pack quarterback would be even more outstanding.

The figure of Starr at the helm of the Packers was a legendary sight.

Bart passed for over 24,718 yards in sixteen incredible years at Green Bay.

Perhaps his greatest moment came in the '67 NFL title game, a repeat against Dallas. The match was played in Arctic conditions and became known as the Ice Bowl.

With thirteen seconds to go, Green Bay were three points behind and stood at fourth and goal on the Cowboy one-yard line. Starr had already thrown two TDs and, on this final drive, had kept his head while all around him were in danger of losing theirs. On fourth and 1, Coach Lombardi decided against a game-tying field goal and overtime — instead, he told Starr to call a quarterback sneak which would win the game outright. Such responsibility is only given to the great players and Bart proved his worth by diving over to put the Pack into Super Bowl II. Once there, Starr again won the MVP honour as the Packers beat Oakland. No quarterback in history had ever won so many titles.

Some experts actually doubted the ability of the man who achieved all those victories because he never had big numbers (his largest passing yardage for one season was only 2,433 in 1962). But Starr led the league in passing three times. He wasn't just the arm of a master team, Starr was the brains and he survived sixteen hectic seasons. Injuries began to strike him more frequently near the end of his career and in 1971 he called it a day.

Starr came back to Green Bay as head coach for nine uneventful seasons, however he couldn't bring back the great years. But, for a seventeenth round draft pick, Starr had already exceeded everybody's expectations by a long way.

★★★ Bart Starr ★★★

Quarterback. 6ft 1in, 200 lb. Born in Montgomery, Alabama, 9 January 1934. Attended University of Alabama. 1956-71 Green Bay Packers.

Passing statistics

Year	Attempts	Competitions	Percentage passes completed	Yards	Touch-down	Interceptions
1956	44	24	54.5	325	2	3
1957	215	117	54.4	1,459	8	10
1958	157	78	49.7	875	3	12
1959	134	70	52.2	972	6	7
1960	172	98	57.0	1,358	4	8
1961	295	172	58.3	2,418	16	16
1962	285	178	62.5	2,433	12	9
1963	244	132	54.1	1,355	15	10
1964	272	163	55.9	2,144	15	4
1965	251	140	55.8	2,055	16	9
1966	251	156	62.2	2,257	14	3
1967	210	115	54.8	1,823	9	17
1968	171	109	63.7	1,617	15	8
1969	148	92	62.2	1,161	9	6
1970	255	140	54.9	1,645	8	13
1971	45	24	53.3	286	0	3
Totals	**3,149**	**1,808**	**57.4**	**24,718**	**152**	**138**

Rushing: 247 attempts, 1,308 yards, 5.3 yard average and 15 touchdowns.

Roger Staubach
The Artful Dodger
the master of the two-minute drill

In the seventies' decade, Roger Staubach *was* the Dallas Cowboys. The ex-Naval Midshipman ruled the field like an Admiral surveying the scene of a conflict. His touch was delicate, his leadership unquestioned, his impact devastating.

In January 1971, the Cowboys reached their first Super Bowl. Second-year Staubach watched helpless from the bench as Baltimore won the trophy 16-13. A year later the Cowboys reached their second Super Bowl. This time the opposition (Miami) watched helplessly as Staubach ripped them up 24-3 and became the game's MVP. That just about sums up how good he was. Staubach was one of those players who make a difference. For nine seasons he made the difference at Dallas and the team hasn't been the same since he left.

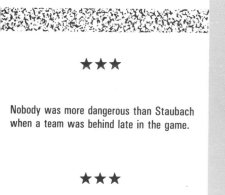

★★★

Nobody was more dangerous than Staubach when a team was behind late in the game.

★★★

He had a never-say-die attitude which could pull the whole club from the brink of terrible defeat. Time and again Staubach used the last minutes of a game to his advantage, to scrape an unlikely victory. Losing wasn't something that Dallas did an awful lot of with him around.

Before Staubach turned pro, he made his name in the Navy team where he won the Heisman Trophy as a mere junior. He then served his country for four years which included a term in Vietnam. He didn't join up with Dallas until 1969 when he was 27 years old. Two seasons of battling with big-game QB Craig Morton postponed his effect on the team. Eventually, after the Super Bowl V disappointment, he was made starter in 1971 when his arrow-straight passes and skilful scrambling helped win Dallas 'The Big One', 24-3 over Miami.

'The Artful Dodger', as he became known, continued to give the Cowboys the edge that they never had before. But another trip to the Super Bowl after the 1975 season led to Staubach meeting his nemesis, Terry Bradshaw of Pittsburgh. Like an Ali-Frazer fight, the two quarterback heavyweights would meet in some classic encounters. However, it was Bradshaw, not Staubach, who always carried off the ultimate prize.

In Super Bowl X the Dallas passer was intercepted three times on the way to a 21-17 loss versus the Steelers. Then three years later Dallas and Pittsburgh lined up again for what is now judged to be the best ever Super Bowl.

The Steelers were 35-17 ahead when Staubach almost brought off the comeback of the century. He threw a seven-yard TD pass with less than $2\frac{1}{2}$ minutes to go and then staged a nine-play drive which ended in another touchdown (this one after Dallas had recovered an onside kick).

Only a man with the brain and coolness of Staubach could have done so much in such a short time. Dallas failed to recover a second onside kick and ended up 35-31 losers, but their quarterback had confirmed his position as a master technician and executor of plays.

Those two losses to Pittsburgh came either side of a happier occasion when the Cowboys beat Denver in Super Bowl XII. On that day Staubach completed 17 of 25 passes for 183 yards and one TD.

After the second Super Bowl loss to the Steelers, Staubach had only one more year in the NFL — yet it was the year that Dallas

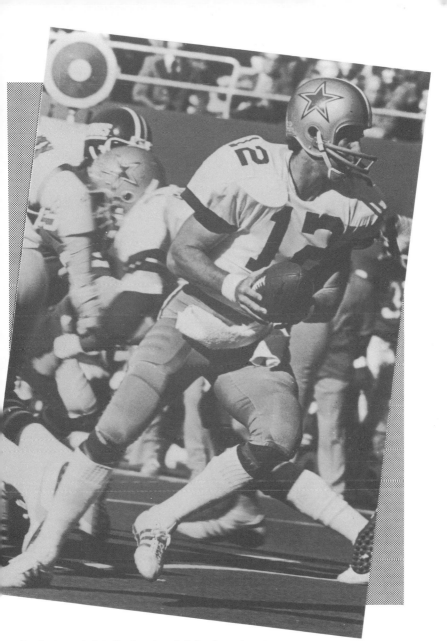

Staubach watched the Cowboys lose their first Super Bowl from the bench as a young back-up, but led them to Super Bowl VI victory a year later.

became known as 'America's Team'. The name came from the title of a highlight video from the previous season. Staubach was the epitome of 'America's Team' just as he was an epitome of America itself.

He was a clean-cut, ex-serviceman who stood over six feet tall and had leadership qualities to inspire men and crush enemies. His last-minute heroics during many Dallas victories were testimony to these attributes.

From 1971 (when Staubach became a starter) to 1979, Dallas won two Super Bowls, six divisional titles and only missed the play-offs once.

Staubach's own record was equally stunning with over 22,000 yards passing 153 TDs and a rating of 83.4 which put him high in the all-time quarterback rankings.

Staubach's teammate Mike Ditka (later head coach at Chicago) summed up the quality of his quarterback. 'There's no such word as "can't" for Roger Staubach. You tell him that and he'll go out and prove you wrong.'

★★★　Roger Staubach　★★★

Quarterback. 6ft 3in, 202 lb. Born in Silverton, Ohio, 5 February 1942. Attended Navy College. 1969-79 Dallas Cowboys.

Passing statistics

Year	Attempts	Completions	Yards	Interceptions	Touchdowns
1969	47	23	421	2	1
1970	82	44	542	8	2
1971	211	126	1,882	4	15
1972	20	9	98	2	0
1973	286	179	2,428	15	23
1974	360	190	2,552	15	11
1975	348	198	2,666	16	17
1976	369	208	2,715	11	14
1977	361	210	2,620	9	18
1978	413	231	3,190	16	25
1979	461	267	3,586	11	27
Totals	**2,958**	**1,685**	**22,700**	**109**	**153**

Jan Stenerud
The Norseman
a kicker with accuracy and longevity

The job of an NFL kicker is one of the most precarious in sport. Jan Stenerud was one of the few men to turn the position into a cast-iron certainty. Over nineteen straight-down-the-middle seasons, the former Norweigian international ski jumper kicked more field goals than any man in pro football history. He set plenty of records, won dozens of last-gasp games and seemed to get better as he got older.

In his penultimate season, Stenerud made the Pro Bowl for the fourth time after performances like a 53-yarder with two seconds left to beat Tampa Bay. All that pressure, all those held-breaths, all those yards to cope with three weeks before your 42nd birthday.

Curiosity had gotten Stenerud started as a kicker in his junior year at Montana State University. He was running up and down the football stadium steps when he gave in to the temptation to join some kickers on the field below. He tried the straight-on method which was then the only style used in the colleges, but he sprayed the ball everywhere. Then struck one ball like a soccer corner kick — the effect was stunning and Stenerud left the sport of ski jumping forever. The Norseman signed a pro contract with the Kansas City Chiefs who were among the top clubs in the new American Football League.

His first season saw Stenerud gain AFL All-Star status, but in the close-season he heard that the Chiefs coaches were scouting in Europe for kickers. Such contrary actions on the part of his employers would test the temperament of any athlete, and the calmness that Stenerud showed making so many field goals was being called into action off the field. 'A kicker's toughest games are in training camp and pre-season just to keep his place in the team,' he said once.

Stenerud beat off all opponents and by his third season was playing in Super Bowl IV. The Chiefs played Minnesota who scored a total of seven points. Stenerud alone scored 11 (including a field

Dawson holds, Stenerud kicks and Kansas City are
on their way to Super Bowl IV glory.

goal of 48 yards which has been one of the Super Bowl's most
lasting records).

As the Chiefs' fortunes sank, their placekicker remained among the leaders of his profession. For thirteen years he was their most dependable performer, leading the league in field goals three times. Finally, at the age of 38, the Norseman stood down for a younger man. However, his fitness was never in doubt and he eventually signed for Green Bay mid-way through the next season.

Just a stop-gap, some said. Stenerud defied such words and enjoyed some of his best periods. In 1982, he set a league record for field goal accuracy with 22 three-pointers out of 24 attempts, a 91.67 percent success rate. A year later Stenerud turned a Monday night football TV programme into his own benefit show. In that one game he proved beyond all doubt how valuable a good kicker can be to a team.

Again Tampa Bay were the victims when Stenerud opened his account with a field goal that equalled the all-time record of 335 successes set by George Blanda.

His second field goal of the night gave him the all-time record on his own. His third took the game into overtime. His fourth won it. The Packers had won 12-9 and Stenerud had scored all their points.

But placekicking is a funny business indeed, for Jan gave way to a younger man for the second time in his career and went to the Vikings.

Minnesota didn't mind because the real-life Viking had a Pro Bowl year. His very first kick for the Vikes was a mighty 54-yarder, just as it had been for the Chiefs in his rookie season. After one more season with Minnesota, the Norseman finally retired with his place in football history secure.

Besides the all-time field goal record, Stenerud finished as second all-time scorer with 1,699 career points.

In those nineteen seasons, the Norseman survived severe lows before he got nationwide attention. In 1971, Kansas City went into overtime against Miami in an AFC play-off game. It would be the longest game in pro football history up to that date. The first chance of extra-time victory fell to the Chiefs kicker, but Stenerud's 42 yard attempt was blocked. In the depths of post-match depression, Stenerud considered retiring immediately. However, the equable temperament that a good kicker needs reversed such thoughts and he went on to complete an illustrious career.

The pressure-cooker art of placekicking requires an unusual talent. It can be a lonely life, set apart from teammates, with the outcome of a game resting on one swing of your leg.

Before he took up kicking footballs, Stenerud was a Norweigian international ski jumper.

Life played a bizarre trick on Stenerud when it led him to make a living at a sport he once described as 'a lot of overweight people running into each other'.

Jan Stenerud overcame those problems for nineteen high class seasons. A Norwegian kicking an American football field goal soccer-style must have been a rare sight back in the mid-sixties. By the mid-eighties, it was one of the most dependable sights the NFL had ever seen.

★★★   Jan Stenerud   ★★★

Kicker. 6ft 2in, 190 lb. Born Fetsund, Norway, on 26 November 1942. Attended Montana State University. 1967-79 Kansas City Chiefs, 1980-83 Green Bay Packers, 1984-85 Minnesota Vikings.

Kicking statistics

Year	Field-goals	Percentage of field-goals scored	Extra points	Extra points percentage	Points
+ 1967	21-36	58.3	45-45	10.0	108
+ 1968	30-40	75.0	39-40	97.5	129
+ 1969	27-35	77.1	38-38	10.0	119
+ 1970	30-42	71.4	26-26	10.0	116
+ 1971	26-44	59.1	32-32	10.0	110
+ 1972	21-36	58.3	32-32	10.0	95
+ 1973	24-38	63.2	21-23	91.3	93
+ 1974	17-24	70.8	24-26	92.3	75
+ 1975	22-32	68.8	30-31	96.8	96
+ 1976	21-38	55.3	27-33	81.8	90
+ 1977	8-18	44.4	27-28	96.4	51
+ 1978	20-30	66.7	25-26	96.2	85
+ 1979	12-23	52.2	28-29	96.6	64
* 1980	3-5	60.0	3-3	10.0	12
* 1981	22-24	91-7	35-35	10.0	101
* 1982	13-18	72.2	25-27	92.6	64
* 1983	21-26	80.8	52-52	10.0	115
● 1984	20-23	87.0	30-31	96.8	90
● 1985	15-26	57.6	41-43	95.3	86
Totals	**573-558**	**67.1**	**580-600**	**96.6**	**1,699**

+ with Kansas City
* with Green Bay
● with Minnesota Vikings

Fran Tarkenton
Fran the Scram
king of the scramblers

Some quarterbacks are famed passers. Others make their names as hand-off merchants. Fran Tarkenton invented a third category — the scrambler.

He became known as 'Fran the Scram'. It would be unfair to list his quality as a runner as his only one — but it's always the one that Tarkenton is most remembered for. He's still listed as the rusher with the top seasonal average in the Minnesota Vikings all-time list (5.6 yards per carry) and he rushed for about 3,000 yards during a career which spanned eighteen seasons with both the Vikings (during two separate periods) and the New York Giants.

The reason for his scrambling antics was only that he wanted to pass much more than run. So, Fran would bide his time. No three-steps-back-and-pass routines for him. If a receiver wasn't open when Tarkenton reached the pocket, then he'd simply roam around until the guy got free. He had a sixth sense which told him when the pass rushing linemen were breaking through. As soon as he felt the pressure, Fran would shimmy out of their way and wait for his target to shake of his man.

That run-around style allowed Tarkenton to get off an astonishing 6,467 pass attempts. Even more astonishing, perhaps, was the fact that he connected with well over half, 3,686 to be precise.

More statistics bring more amazement. Tarkenton's passing totted up 47,003 yards of offense (33,098 with the Vikings) and 342 touchdowns. All those four marks are NFL records — most of them by miles. He attempted 1,400 more than the no 2, completed 800 more than the next QB, gained almost 7,000 yards more than his runner-up and scored 52 more touchdowns.

Tarkenton certainly left his mark on the league. The only surprise is that he wasn't inducted into the Hall of Fame in his first year of eligibility (1984), but got the vote a year later instead.

Back in 1961, though, Minnesota knew they were getting a star of the future when they drafted Tarkenton from the University of

Tarkenton was definitely his own
man. He quarelled many times with Vikings first coach Norm Van Brocklin.

Georgia. It was the Vikings' very first year in the NFL. The team was
made up of throwaway players from other clubs plus college new
boys like Tarkenton. All the problems of setting up a new franchise
never affected the Tarkenton confidence which was to become
well-known in later years. By the end of the inaugural season, Fran
had both hands on the starting job.

He made his point early — in the first game, in fact. Tarkenton
replaced a veteran starter in the second quarter, threw four TDs and
ran in the fifth himself. But tension soon began to rise between him
and coach Norm Van Brocklin. The Vikes weren't exactly setting the

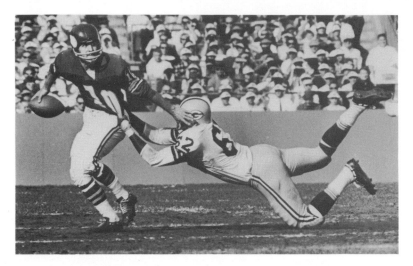
Fran lives up to his nickname here on a mad scramble as he searches out a receiver.

NFL ablaze, and the two men disagreed about Fran's less-than-classic style. At times they hardly spoke to each other at all.

Someone had to give and, in the end, it turned out to be both of them. Before the '67 season, Tarkenton was traded to the Giants and Van Brocklin resigned. Fran missed the start of new coach Bud Grant's assault on the league — but he would return.

The advantage of Tarkenton in New York was that a mega-sized personality could perform in the media capital of the world.

Fran's scrambling scenes were given a broader canvas thanks to the important home town press corps, who reported on its uniqueness if not its success.

His trade had cost NY four high draft choices. They couldn't win with Tarkenton and their veterans and found it hard to rebuild without top draft picks.

Fans in Minnesota often wondered how their team would have performed if Fran hadn't left when Grant arrived. Tarkenton's replacement, Joe Kapp, got involved in a contract dispute and few observers were surprised when the dreams of those Vikings fans came true. The Vikes got Fran back in 1972.

During Tarkenton's absence, Minnesota had appeared in Super Bowl IV and lost. His return sparked hope of another Super Bowl appearance — and this time a win.

Tarkenton's NFL records for attempts, completions, yardage and passing touchdowns could last forever.

In fact Fran led the Vikes to three Super Bowls — nos VII, VIII and XI — but all of them ended in defeat. It wasn't all Tarkenton's fault that Minnesota lost three championships, but a star of his magnitude had to accept a fair measure of the responsibility. He came up against Miami in their post-perfect season, Pittsburgh at the start of their dominant era and the Oakland Raiders on a day when John Madden and his men could do no wrong.

In the 1977 draft, Minnesota picked QB Tommy Kramer in the first round. The writing was on the wall for the older man. That last Super Bowl defeat came after the '76 season, Tarkenton broke his leg in '77 and finally retired after the '78 campaign to become a TV analyst.

It was a diginified way to go for a man who sometimes turned the gridiron into a scene from a Keystone Kops movie. His record scrambling time was 28 seconds. Pittsburgh lineman 'Mean' Joe

Greene tells this story about one time he sacked Tarkenton: 'I kept chasing him and when I finally hit him, I didn't realize he'd thrown the ball five minutes before!'

Tarkenton was a thrilling player who had the confidence and the ability to throw at any time — even from his own end zone — plus an unheard of quality at that time to scramble. There'll probably never be another quarterback quite like him — a one-man throwing and running mean machine.

★★★ **Fran Tarkenton** ★★★

Quarterback. 6ft 0in, 185 lb. Born in Richmond, Virginia, 3 February 1940. Attended University of Georgia. 1961-66 and 1972-78 Minnesota Vikings, 1967-71 New York Giants.

Passing statistics

Year	Attempts	Completions	Percentage passes completed	Yards	Touch-downs	Interceptions
*1961	280	157	56.1	1,997	18	17
*1962	329	163	49.5	2,595	22	25
*1963	297	170	57.2	2,311	15	15
*1964	306	171	55.9	2,506	22	11
*1965	329	171	52.0	2,609	19	11
*1966	358	192	53.6	2,561	17	16
+1967	377	204	54.1	3,088	29	19
+1968	337	182	54.0	2,555	21	12
+1969	409	220	53.8	2,918	23	8
+1970	389	219	56.3	2,779	19	12
+1971	386	226	58.5	2,567	11	21
*1972	378	215	56.9	2,651	18	13
*1973	274	169	61.7	2,113	15	7
*1974	351	199	56.7	2,598	17	12
*1975	425	273	64.2	2,994	25	13
*1976	412	255	61.9	2,961	17	8
*1977	258	155	60.1	1,734	9	14
*1978	572	345	60.3	3,468	25	32
Totals	**6,467**	**3,686**	**57.0**	**47,003**	**342**	**266**

* with Minnesota Vikings
+ with New York Giants

Rushing: 675 attempts, 3,674 yards, 5.4 yard average, 32 touchdowns.

Jim Thorpe
Red Indian
Superman

perhaps the world's greatest ever athlete

Wa-Tho-Huck was the Red Indian name given to Jim Thorpe at his birth. It meant Bright Path. And such words described his career as an athlete. In fact, his could have been the brightest path of all. As a sportsmen he was nothing short of a phenomenon. His talents spanned many sports and he conquered them all. He had awesome natural strength for his 6ft 1in, 190 lb frame, he ran like the wind and his body absorbed a mountain of punishment without ever seeming to bruise.

All these qualities and more were to take the worlds of American football, baseball and athletics by storm. Had the famous letter C on the front of his Canton football jersey been replaced with an S for Superman then nobody would have questioned it.

Thorpe joined the world of pro football after being tagged as the world's greatest all-round athlete.

It was running with the football at which Thorpe excelled, but he did almost everything with equal brilliance including kicking.

Perhaps the ultimate accolade was bestowed on him before he ever played professional football. It happened at the 1912 Olympic Games in Stockholm, Sweden. Thorpe the wonder man had just won gold medals in both the pentathlon and decathlon — the five and ten-sport individual disciplines. 'You are the greatest athlete in the world,' King Gustav V of Sweden told Thorpe. 'Thanks, King' replied the unassuming hero. This story would become as legendary as its main protagonist but it was to have several twists before it was completed.

Thorpe had to return his medals when an Olympic committee

Thorpe's teams included a team of American Indians based in Oorang, Ohio. They folded after one season.

discovered he'd earned $2 a game playing minor league baseball two years before. It was a trifling breach of the amateur rules of the Olympics and it took seventy years of campaigning for that decision to be reversed. Eventually the medals were presented to his family in 1982 — 29 years after Thorpe had died.

Nevertheless, no one could take away Thorpe's achievement. A year after the Olympics he played in baseball's World Series (their version of the Super Bowl) before being signed for the footballing Canton Bulldogs in 1915 at $250 a game — an astronomical figure in those days.

Thorpe was more popular than popcorn and guaranteed that national attention was focused on the growing sport of football. He was even made president of the sport's first national pro league in 1920 (it preceded the NFL by a year). It wasn't Thorpe's statesman qualities the league wanted — it was just his name. That name guaranteed crowds and what they came to see was raw power.

Thorpe played football with unmitigating savagery. When he carried the ball he bludgeoned into opponents like a rogue elephant. When he tackled it was with lion-like ferocity. Added to this he could pass, punt, block and kick — all with equal brilliance.

After the Bulldogs, he roamed to the Cleveland Indians, Oorang Indians, Rock Island Independents, New York Giants and Chicago Cardinals. None of those teams had any success and some even collapsed after Thorpe's departure. Unfortunately his collapse was also coming soon. Those comet-high days of Thorpe's early successes were to be clouded by a dramatic tailing off.

At 40 he was still taking the punishment but had become a sad figure past his prime. Drink and gambling began to take over even before he retired in 1928. He drifted into and out of undignified manual jobs and even to Hollywood where he picked up a few dollars as an extra or a football expert.

Thorpe's death in 1953 at the age of 64 was probably a relief. After sport left his life there was nothing that could fill it. Yet despite this unhappy demise he is still recognized as a truly remarkable man.

In 1950 he was voted as the best American athlete of the half century while in 1963 he became a charter member of the Pro Football Hall of Fame. The pudgy-faced football warrior from the Sac and Fox Red Indian tribe has become immortal.

★★★   Jim Thorpe   ★★★

Halfback. 6ft 1in, 190 lb. Born in Prague, Oklahoma, 28 May, 1888. Died 28 March, 1953. Attended Carlisle University. 1920 Canton Bulldogs, 1921 Cleveland Indians, 1922-23 Oorang Indians, 1923 Toledo Maroons, 1924 Rock Island Independents, 1925 New York Giants, 1926 Canton Bulldogs, 1928 Chicago Cardinals.

Johnny Unitas
All-American Hero

the coolest man ever in the quarterback spot

The Johnny Unitas story is football's version of the American dream. A young man attends a small town college; his football ability seems unspectacular and the NFL rejects him; later he is plucked from a semi-pro team and thrust into a starring role; he plays with such skill and courage that he takes the league by storm and carves his name in letters at least ten feet high in the annals of pro football.

It sounds like a fairy story, but it's all true and it happened to Johnny Unitas. In eighteen seasons and 211 games between 1956 and 1973, he set every passing record worth setting and played a leading role in the first gridiron game to capture the imagination of a nation.

Unitas was born in Pittsburgh in 1933 and grew into a gawky youth who went to college at unfashionable Louisville. He was drafted in the ninth round by his home town team, but the Steelers cut him in training camp. Disillusioned, Johnny drifted into semi-pro football earning just six dollars a game. A year later (1956) a phone call from the Baltimore Colts brought him back into the NFL. He was signed as a second-string, but an injury to the starting QB soon took him into the team.

Within two season the Colts (still only six years old) were NFL champions. Unitas was one of the main reasons why. For a phone call costing a few cents, Baltimore had rescued the career of a man who they soon realized was invaluable. Unitas thrived on the pressure of being a field lieutenant and his 6ft-1in, 195 lb frame would stand with unbelievable calm in the suicide spot they call the quarterback pocket. He developed a kind of radar for his receivers who would feature men like Raymond Berry and John Mackey.

His spikey crew cut and old-fashioned high-top shoes didn't give him a flashy on-the-field personality. Instead, he concentrated on doing his job. It was something he did better than just about anyone else. His time to prove it came in the 1958 NFL championship game

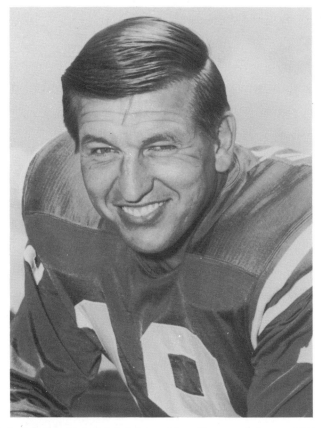

Unitas' old fashioned hair style belied one of the gridiron game's foremost thinkers.

against the New York Giants. It's probably the most famous game in pro football history.

An audience of millions on TV watched spellbound as Unitas moved the Colts 66 yards for a game-tying TD near the end of normal time. When the match moved into overtime, Unitas moved his team into overdrive. He was just 25 years old on that day when he moved the Colts into the Giants end zone for victory. It was the sport's first sudden-death championship. The television millions and America itself got a new national sport that day and Unitas was its hero. The following season, Unitas took his team to a second NFL title. He passed for two TDs and ran one in himself in another

Standing cool in the pocket and getting the pass off at the last minute was a Unitas trademark.

In pro football's most famous game (Colts versus Giants NFL title match of 1958) Unitas is seen about to rifle another pass downfield.

win over the Giants.

Apart from those two glory days, Unitas played in two Super Bowls. However, these experiences were troubled ones, both marred with injury. In Super Bowl III, he sat on the sidelines because a regular season injury had kept him out of the team for a while. His back-up Earl Morrall then kept him out when Johnny was almost back to full fitness and, in the big game, Unitas watched as his 18-point favourite Colts slid to defeat. He saw some desperate fourth quarter action, but it was too late.

Two years later, the situation was virtually reversed. Johnny started the game only to take a hit near half-time that left him holding the side of his body. He didn't return. However, Morrall came in and a victory was secured. How strange that such a marvellous quarterback was never able to perform at his best on the greatest football stage in the world.

By then speculation had already begun that Unitas could no longer throw the long pass. His interception total was beginning to creep higher and two years later he left the Colts for an ill-fated stay at San Diego. He knew things were wrong and he soon quit the game.

For eighteen years he graced football fields with skill and bravery. His list of injuries during that career had included a punctured lung. Unitas was never lacking in the necessary qualities: when the experts looked back at his seasons at the top, they praised his unique ability to stay cool under the severest pressure. It was something all his contemporaries admired. They thought of him as, simply, the best.

His story was a classic rags-to-riches tale, straight out of a comic strip, a real Cinderella kid. The phone call that plucked him out of obscurity had cost about 50 cents — a small price to pay for genius.

★★★   Johnny Unitas   ★★★

Quarterback. 6ft 1in, 195 lb. Born in Pittsburgh, Pennsylvania, 7 may 1933. University of Louisville. 1956-72 Baltimore Colts, 1973 San Diego Chargers.

Passing statistics

Year	Attempts	Completions	Percentage passes completed	Yards	Touch-down	Interceptions
* 1956	198	110	55.6	1,498	9	10
* 1957	301	172	57.1	2,550	24	17
* 1958	263	136	51.7	2.007	19	7
* 1959	367	193	52.6	2,899	32	14
* 1960	378	190	50.3	3,099	25	24
* 1961	420	229	54.5	2,990	16	24
* 1962	389	222	57.1	2,967	23	23
* 1963	410	237	57.8	3,481	20	12
* 1964	305	158	51.8	2,824	19	6
* 1965	282	164	58.2	2,530	23	12
* 1966	348	195	56.0	2,743	22	24
* 1967	436	255	58.5	3,428	20	16
* 1968	32	11	34.4	139	2	4
* 1969	327	178	54.4	2,342	12	20
* 1970	321	166	51.7	2,213	14	18
* 1971	176	92	52.3	942	3	9
* 1972	157	88	56.1	1,111	4	6
+ 1973	76	34	44.7	471	3	7
Totals	**5,186**	**2,830**	**54.1**	**40,239**	**290**	**253**

* with Baltimore Colts
+ with San Diego Chargers

Paul Warfield
The Speedster
a major threat even when he didn't get the ball

Imagine having a guy on your team who scored a touchdown every fifth pass that he caught. That woud be something, wouldn't it? That would, in fact, have been Paul Warfield. In thirteen NFL seasons, Warfield was the premier deep threat in the league. He consistently averaged over twenty yards per catch and his career centred on the quality of those receptions rather than the quantity.

This guy was quite some athlete, whose graceful pass patterns so often ended with a leap, a catch and a touchdown. It was stirring stuff, indeeed. Yet, to have such a player on your team provided more than just his receiving. Warfield was more often used as the decoy either for a run or a pass to another receiver. It was a role that one so great has to accept — that he's almost as effective when he doesn't receive the ball as when he does. A man of Warfield's calibre takes the heat off everyone else. The man himself found this fact hard to appreciate and it would lead to a major mistake in his glittering career.

Nevertheless, everything began in impressive fashion. Warfield was drafted by his home state team, Cleveland. He'd been a football and track star at Ohio State where he was a long jumper capable of exceeding 26 ft and top Buckeye receiver. Yet, Paul doubted his ability to adapt to the pros. 'The Browns in 1964 had Jim Brown and so many other great players that I was in awe of them,' he said.

Such misgivings proved groundless as he enjoyed a blockbusting rookie year. He caught 52 passes (a figure he would never beat) for 920 yards and nine touchdowns. The Browns even went on to win the NFL title in Warfield's first season (he was mainly in his decoy role in that game), but in season no 2 he broke a shoulder which kept him out for ten weeks.

Warfield won many admirers during six years at Cleveland. Coaches praised him for matching speed with preciseness and safe hands. The Browns fans adored him. But the seemingly-perfect situation was disturbed by Cleveland's desperate need for a

Warfield (left) had five years at Miami. Here he poses with fellow receiver Marlin Briscoe.

If a catch needed speed, deception
and concentration, then Warfield was the best man for the job.

quarterback. In 1970, the team's management decided they would
have to trade a player for a top draft pick. Surprisingly they chose to
trade Warfield.

The move was a great disappointment to Paul who was soon on
his way to a poor Miami team. However, the arrival of coach Don
Shula helped lift his gloom. In his first year as a Dolphin, Warfield hit
his best ever pass yardage average of 25.1 yards. Shula used him
sparingly that year, but Warfield saw more of the football in his next
season as Miami made the Super Bowl. Unfortunately, on the day,
Dallas beat them soundly 24-3. Warfield caught four passes for 39
yards.

By 1972, Miami had one of *the* great teams. However, the
Dolphins relied on a ground game for a controlled offense with
Warfield seldom brought into play. Paul wasn't happy with being
under-used, but there were benefits as the team went to a perfect
17-0 season. They won the Super Bowl again the following season.

Warfield wasn't used as a pass target as
often as he would have liked, but he still caught 427 footballs.

In those two major games, Paul was given just five passes to catch.

Feeling undervalued, Paul was tempted to join the World Football League in 1975 for a six-figure fee. Ten unmemorable games later, his team, the Memphis Southmen, and the league itself folded. Warfield was left in a no man's land. However, Cleveland made sure his career didn't end there by re-signing him, much to Paul's delight.

He must have been even more delighted to find that the Browns' receivers coach was Hall-of-Famer Raymond Berry who paid Warfield this compliment: 'One of Paul's greatest assets is the attention he draws to himself and away from our other receivers'. Paul's final two seasons at Cleveland showed that he was still to be feared, but by 1977 it was time to finish playing at the age of 35.

Seven Pro Bowl appearances, two Super Bowl rings and one NFL championship were the major team honours that Paul Warfield won and, though he felt under-employed, Warfield was a real team player.

A true speedster of Warfield's quality can change a game in an instant and he often did with some flashy, fluid moves and secure handling. Every opposing team had to double-team Warfield because he was so special, but he learned to beat even this kind of heavy traffic. It was something that even his own quarterbacks found hard to believe. Miami's Bob Griese claimed Warfield completely altered his attitude as a quarterback: 'I'd been taught not to throw into double coverage, but he showed me he could beat it'. If only more quarterbacks had believed more in Paul Warfield than their natural instincts, the man could have pulled in the volume of catches that such a talent deserved.

★★★ Paul Warfield ★★★

Wide Receiver. 6ft 0in, 188 lb. Born in Warren, Ohio, 28 November 1942. Attended Ohio State University. 1964-69 and 1976-77 Cleveland Browns, 1970-74 Miami Dolphins, 1975 Memphis Southmen.

Receiving statistics

Year	Receipts	Yards	Average	Touchdowns
* 1964	52	920	17.7	9
* 1965	3	30	10.0	0
* 1966	36	741	20.6	5
* 1967	32	702	21.9	8
* 1968	50	1,067	21.3	12
* 1969	42	886	21.1	10
+ 1970	28	703	25.1	6
+ 1971	43	996	23.2	11
+ 1972	29	606	20.9	3
+ 1973	29	514	17.7	11
+ 1974	27	536	19.9	2
● 1975	25	422	16.9	3
* 1976	38	613	16.1	6
* 1977	18	251	13.9	2
Total	**427**	**8,565**	**20.1**	**85**

* with Cleveland Browns
+ with Miami Dolphins
● with Memphis Southmen

Rushing: 22 attempts, 204 yards, 9.3 yard average and 0 touchdowns.